teach®
yourself

planning your
wedding

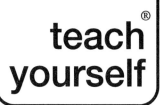

planning your
wedding
christine williams
and dianne ffitch

For UK order enquiries: please contact Bookpoint Ltd, 130 Milton Park, Abingdon, Oxon OX14 4SB. Telephone: +44 (0) 1235 827720. Fax: +44 (0) 1235 400454. Lines are open from 09.00–18.00, Monday to Saturday, with a 24-hour message answering service. Details about our titles and how to order are available at www.teachyourself.co.uk

For USA order enquiries: please contact McGraw-Hill Customer Services, PO Box 545, Blacklick, OH 43004-0545, USA. Telephone: 1-800-722-4726. Fax: 1-614-755-5645.

For Canada order enquiries: please contact McGraw-Hill Ryerson Ltd, 300 Water St, Whitby, Ontario L1N 9B6, Canada. Telephone: 905 430 5000. Fax: 905 430 5020.

Long-renowned as the authoritative source for self-guided learning – with more than 30 million copies sold worldwide – the *Teach Yourself* series includes over 300 titles in the fields of languages, crafts, hobbies, busines, computing and education.

British Library Cataloguing in Publication Data:
A catalogue record for this title is available from The British Library.

Library of Congress Catalog Card Number: On file

First published in UK 2003 by Hodder Headline, 338 Euston Road, London, NW1 3BH.

First published in US 2003 by Contemporary Books, A Division of the McGraw Hill Companies, 1 Prudential Plaza, 130 East Randolph Street, Chicago, Illinois 60601 USA.

The 'Teach Yourself' name is a registered trade mark of Hodder & Stoughton Ltd.

Copyright © 2003 Christine Williams and Dianne ffitch

Typeset by Transet Limited, Coventry, England.
Printed in Great Britain for Hodder & Stoughton Educational, a division of Hodder Headline, 338 Euston Road, London NW1 3BH by Cox & Wyman Ltd, Reading, Berkshire.

Hodder Headline's policy is to use papers that are natural, renewable and recyclable products and made from wood grown in sustainable forests. The logging and manufacturing processes are expected to conform to the environmental regulations of the country of origin.

Impression number   10 9 8 7 6 5 4 3 2
Year   2009 2008 2007 2006 2005 2004

contents

acknowledgements

For Paul, my wonderful husband for his love and devotion, and my masterminds – Jackie, Jean and Joan – for their continued support.

Dianne ffitch

For Jason and Fiona, Katherine and David – beautiful brides and handsome grooms, my inspiration, always.

Christine Williams

About the authors

Dianne ffitch has over 20 years of experience organizing hospitality events of all kinds including small but prestigious dinners, office parties, golf days, conferences and corporate and team building events for both local and multi-national companies throughout the UK. She has offered wedding co-ordination services since 1999.

Christine Williams designed and launched events, including conferences, corporate training events and family celebrations for six years.

introduction

Public attitudes towards marriage, today, are very different from those held by previous generations. At its best, marriage is a life-long commitment of love, loyalty and fidelity; a partnership that sustains two people (and their children, if they have them) through joy and pain, success and failure. It is a public declaration of private promises and a reason for celebration and ceremony.

Most of us achieve a marriage which is somewhere between the two extremes of bliss and misery, balancing joy and sadness, happiness and frustrations, knowing that sharing life with someone who cares is a powerful blessing. Still, a successful marriage doesn't just happen and the pressures of modern living are not always conducive to happy ever after.

Even so, marriage is still very much on the agenda for most people and the majority of us take the plunge at some time during our lives. Arranging a wedding can be complicated, frustrating, time consuming and expensive – it is also exciting, entertaining and, occasionally, hilariously funny. The variety of different ways in which we can celebrate the big day itself has never been so wide and changes in the law (1995) mean that it is possible to marry in many more venues than were possible before, adding to the complications!

It is an important day and you want to get it right. This book will help you decide whether a traditional or non-traditional style wedding is what you want, help you organize what needs to be done, and when, and how to plan the budget. Good luck – have a marvellous day!

How to use this book

We, the authors and the publisher, hope that this book will be helpful to everyone who is about to become involved in a wedding, no matter what role they are to play. Primarily, however, it is addressed to those who are directly involved in making plans and/or those doing things on the day. Most couples take control of their own wedding preparations, planning the day with friends and family as advisors and supporters. There are still a few, however, who choose the traditional way where the bride and her mother make the decisions, the bride's father pays the bills and the groom turns up on the day! Whatever suits your way of life and circumstances is fine.

In 1995 the law on wedding venues changed. Before this, the only place a wedding ceremony could take place, in order to be valid in British law, was in a church, chapel, synagogue or temple (of any denomination recognized in law as a bone fide religion) or a register office. Now, any place that is granted a licence may host civil ceremonies and it is sometimes possible to arrange a religious blessing, after the civil proceedings, at the same place. Much depends on the faith, of course, and the flexibility of the local minister, priest or preacher. Almost everyone, however, whether directly connected or not, will freely offer advice and assistance so, with all the help available, it is easy to understand how so many planners hold the view that arranging a wedding is fairly straightforward. All one needs is a telephone, a telephone directory and a little time, right? Wrong! A wedding is the largest and most expensive event that most people will ever arrange and we have all heard the old proverb about too many cooks. It often proves to be far more complicated than expected, leading to all sorts of strange, and occasionally comic, results.

> Arranging a wedding for their respective children, two sets of parents could not agree where the reception was to be held – in the village where the bride's family lived, or just down the road, in the groom's family's village. It was finally, and amicably, agreed that there would be two receptions, one in each village, and guests would move between the two as they wished. This original solution kept the peace. The reception went on for two days and the newly-weds slipped away to start their honeymoon, unnoticed, quite early in the proceedings.

If there is any secret at all in arranging a successful wedding, it lies in careful planning, careful budgeting and taking the time to be thorough. Most weddings take between nine and twelve months to plan, not because a long lead time is strictly necessary, but because most weddings are organized in the chief planner's spare time, with a few minutes here and an hour or so there. Nevertheless, an early start ensures more choice and fewer hurried decisions, even if you employ a professional wedding planner.

This book takes you through what needs to be done in a logical order. Read through the chapters carefully and you should find that everything is catered for.

It is easy to forget, amidst the excitement of shopping, planning and preparation, that marriage is also a solemn commitment and that the wedding day is just the beginning of a completely different experience and lifestyle. This book is designed to help you with the former without neglecting the deeper implications of the latter. Most of you will read it for the express purpose of using it to help you plan your own wedding, in which case the authors, the publisher and everyone else who has had a hand in putting this book together, wish you a long and happy marriage.

Couples today very often want to do something personal and of meaning to them – and why not? It is your day to enjoy and remember for the rest of your life.

Although you may get assistance from immediate members of your family, do not lose sight of what you really want.

Above all, do not worry. All brides and grooms have moments of doubt; at some point you will wonder how you are going to cope with all the requirements of organizing your wedding. And behind all the planning that is going on, there is the certain knowledge that you are about to take one of the most important steps in your life which will affect you for the rest of your days. At some point you may suddenly turn from the perfectly sane individual, into a screaming wreck! However, it will all be worth it in the end. With the help of family and friends, you will have the perfect day that you dream of, with wonderful memories to savour for the rest of your life. This book will assist with its wealth of inspiring ideas. And remember, with careful planning, all things are possible! Be as daring as you like – it's your day!

01

the legal requirements

This chapter deals with the legal aspects of marriage in England and Wales, together with notes on the variations found in Scotland and Ireland and the way the law impacts on faiths other than Christianity. It's not the most exciting of subjects, when you're planning something with all the fizz and bubble of a wedding, but it is vital because, even today, there are some common misconceptions about what is legal and what is simply custom and practice, or vice versa. In this chapter we look at some of the options, explain what must be done to comply with the law, and what can be added by way of celebration and ceremony. If, when you have read the chapter, you are still unsure about anything contact your minister, priest, Citizen's Advice Bureau, registrar or solicitor for help.

The Anglican marriage service says that marriage is 'an honourable estate, instituted of God in the time of man's innocence'. Clearly, then, marriage has a long history and, in most communities, carries the blessings of God (by whatever name the deity is called) as well as that of society in general. In the United Kingdom, the Anglican Church, embodied in the Churches of England and Wales, of Ireland and of Scotland, is the Church of State with the reigning monarch at its head. Because of this unique position, ministers of the Anglican Churches are also registrars and may perform marriage ceremonies that fulfil the legal requirements of the State, integrated into religious custom. In order to have legal validity, marriages celebrated in other faiths and religions must fulfil additional legal requirements.

When the Pope refused to annul the marriage of Henry VIII to his queen, Catherine (of Aragon), Henry took the Church in England out of the Roman Catholic Church and declared himself Head and Defender of the Church in England. He then declared his marriage annulled and promptly married again, to Anne Boleyn. England's Church was still essentially Catholic during the reign of Henry with its character becoming Protestant only under the short reign of his son, Edward. Mary Tudor, Henry's eldest child and daughter of Catherine of Aragon, attempted to reverse the process when she came to the throne after Edward's death. Elizabeth I, Henry's daughter by Anne Boleyn, completed the task her brother had begun when she, in her turn, came to the throne after Mary's death.

What are the legal requirements?

The word 'wedding' originates from the Anglo-Saxon 'wed' which means 'to pledge'. This is what a marriage consists of – each partner making individual pledges. For such pledges to constitute a legal marriage, it has to be a public declaration, witnessed by at least two independent adults.

In order to be legally married within the laws of the United Kingdom you must:

- not be married already to someone else
- not be related by blood, adoption or marriage to each other within certain specific degrees (see page 7)
- be in possession of certain documents
- give notice to the registrar, priest or minister at the right time
- pay the fees
- live in the registration district in which you want to get married, or be marrying someone who lives in that district (minimum residency qualification is 15 days prior to giving notice of the intended marriage to the registrar or minister)
- either have the Banns read (Anglican Church only) or obtain the appropriate certificate
- arrange the ceremony, which has to take place between the hours of 8 a.m. and 6 p.m., in a properly licensed place (the exceptions to this are those performed with a special licence or a Registrar General's licence, or Jewish or Quaker ceremonies)
- have the ceremony performed and registered by a properly licensed person
- have two independent witnesses present at the ceremony
- turn up at the appointed place at the right time
- be of sound mind, understand the nature of the commitment you are making, and not be acting under duress (i.e. you must consent to the marriage)
- as a couple comprise one female and one male by birth
- make sure you collect a copy of the entry in the Registrar's Book of Marriages (the Marriage Certificate) after the ceremony.

The registrar or minister will prompt you on most of this, so don't worry. Have the following documents available, if they apply to you, it will save time:

- birth certificate
- death certificate of spouse (if previously married and now widowed)

- passport (if you are a foreign national)
- decree absolute (if a previous marriage has been dissolved)
- baptismal certificate (if you are marrying in church)
- letter of consent from guardian or parent (if under 18 in England and Wales).

Laws relating to marriage ceremonies in Scotland and Northern Ireland vary a little and these variations are covered on pages 21–23.

Who may marry?

The Christian Churches, both Catholic and Protestant, have traditionally forbidden marriages within certain 'degrees of relationship', which are also enshrined in civil law. Some of these ancient taboos have relaxed a little in modern times but many remain.

Marriages forbidden in law

Most people are aware that they may not marry certain relatives and that these are:

For men	For women
Mother	Father
Grandmother	Grandfather
Daughter	Son
Granddaughter	Grandson
Aunt	Uncle
Niece	Nephew
Sister	Brother
Any person registered at birth as male	Any person registered at birth as female
Daughter-in-law*	Son-in-law*
Mother-in-law*	Father-in-law*
Step-daughter*	Step-son*
Step-sister*	Step-brother*
Adopted sister*	Adopted brother*
Adopted daughter*	Adopted son*

*but see section on relationships where marriage may be possible in certain circumstances.

Many cultures have, throughout history, forbidden marriage between people who are closely connected by blood. Thousands of years before the explosion in our knowledge of genetics, the results of interbreeding were observed, the cause identified and prohibitions enshrined in folk-lore, religion and law. But why a bar on marriage between adoptive relatives? Well, to make distinctions in marriage for adopted people would be to undermine the very reason that adoption laws were formulated in the first place, which was to place adopted people on exactly the same basis as natural children, with no distinction or discrimination in law at all.

Contrary to the view held by many people, there is no bar that prevents cousins marrying each other.

However, marriage between certain step-relatives *is* forbidden in law. If two people are raised as siblings from childhood, living in the same family home, even though they have different parents (as often happens in new families formed by second marriages) they are not permitted to marry each other.

Lastly, two people who were registered as the same gender at birth may not marry each other, no matter what has happened since then. The law has recently, however, been modified to allow recognition of long term commitment within same sex relationships. Registration confers certain rights regarding pensions, property tenancies, inheritance and more. Check with your local law centre, citizen's advice bureau or solicitor to find out more. These rights do not extend, however, to male/female co-habitation. Whilst this might seem illogical at first sight, men and women have the option and choice of marriage, which same sex partners do not.

Relationships where marriage may be possible in certain circumstances

Normally, people who have lived as relatives in the same household are not permitted to marry when adult even though there is no blood relationship. However, there are two sets of circumstances where such a marriage is possible.

The first is when the elder of the two people was over 18 years of age when the step-relationship began, e.g. when their respective parents married, even though the other party may have been much younger.

The second is when the two people have not actually lived together in the same family home (even though they are step-related) *and* both will be 21 or over when the marriage is due to take place. This could be the case when, for example, one of the parties has spent a significant amount of childhood living with their other natural parent or, perhaps, has boarded away at school for several years.

Marriage between a man and his daughter-in-law or mother-in-law, or between a woman and her son-in-law or father-in-law, is possible if both are widowed *and* over the age of 21. If the previous marriage of either or both has been dissolved in divorce and one or both ex-spouses is still alive, or if either of the parties is under 21, then a legal marriage between them is still not possible.

If these criteria are fulfilled then such marriages are valid in English law as long as the parties remain domiciled in territories where English law is recognized. Complications arise, however, if the couple moves abroad. If they become domiciled in a place where such a marriage is not recognized under the law of that country, then it won't be recognized in Britain while the pair remain domiciled abroad, even though it was a perfectly legal marriage when it took place.

It all hinges on the laws of 'domicile'. The couple will be subject to the laws of their new country as a condition of their domiciliary status, even though they may still be British citizens. A doubtful marital status could give rise to all sorts of problems which might even follow such a couple back to the UK, should they subsequently return.

If you believe you might be affected by any of these aspects of the law, and/or may not be sure of the implications, check with a solicitor, or the Superintendent Registrar at your local Registrar of Births, Marriages and Deaths office. A Citizens' Advice Bureau or other legal aid centre might also be able to help, or check the phone book for the address of the local registrar and for solicitors who offer a no-fee consultation interview (and legal aid, if appropriate).

Where and when can you get married?

Most religions and faiths have special places set aside for worship and the performance of certain ceremonies, including marriage. Not all these ceremonies and places are, however, recognized in civil law so a religious marriage ceremony might not necessarily constitute a legal marriage.

To satisfy the law in England, Northern Ireland and Wales, both the place and the person conducting the ceremony must be licensed and the ceremony must be held between the hours of 8 a.m. and 6 p.m. In Scotland, only the registrar needs to be licensed and he or she can perform the ceremony in any suitable building.

Only Anglican ministers and registrars are licensed persons. If a religious ceremony is performed by a minister or priest of any other faith, or branch of a faith, civil registrars must be present to add the legal element to the proceedings.

When you make enquiries about marriage to your minister, priest, rabbi or elder he or she will advise on what civil arrangements are necessary and make sure they are all in order.

Licensed places include most (but not all) places of worship of any branch of a recognized religion (Christian, Muslim, Buddhist, Hindu or Jewish), the local register office and any other premises which has requested, and been granted, the appropriate licence.

Many faiths and religions are represented in the United Kingdom today but their places of worship may not be licensed either because they are not recognized as bone fide religions (e.g., certain New Age sects) or their congregations are too small. In these cases, a civil ceremony must be arranged at the register office or one of the licensed premises described, in addition to, or instead of, the religious ceremony at the place of worship.

Normally a wedding takes place in the parish (church) or district (register office) in which the couple lives but, if they live in different places, both ministers/registrars must be given notice of intent to marry. You can also arrange to marry in another place entirely but you will need to establish residency first. See 'Marrying outside your parish' on page 13.

If you, or your partner, is not domiciled in this country, see 'Marrying a citizen of a foreign country' on page 23.

Documents and residency

In England, Wales, Scotland and Northern Ireland the minimum age for marrying is 16. In Scotland, people of 16 years and over may marry without parental consent but in England, Wales and Northern Ireland those between the ages of 16 and 18 must have the written consent of parent(s) or guardian(s).

Be prepared to show a number of documents to the registrar or minister when you give notice that you want to marry in the parish/district. You should have a birth (or adoption) certificate, a baptismal certificate if you wish to marry in church, the written consent of parents or guardians if you are under 18 and/or a divorce decree absolute/annulment paper or death certificate if there has been a previous marriage. If you are a foreign national, you might be asked to produce your passport and visas.

Before giving notice of your intention to marry to the minister or registrar, you must each have lived in your respective parish or district for 15 clear days and intend to marry in one of them. If you are both foreign nationals, only one of you needs to establish this residency and give notice but the other must be somewhere in the country on the day notice is given.

Details of where to obtain British birth and death certificates are given in Taking it further. Enquiries to obtain a duplicate divorce decree absolute should be addressed to the county court at which the hearing was held, or your local county court if you are not sure which one you should apply to.

All requests should be accompanied with as much detail as possible, including full names, all relevant dates, and so on. There is a charge for these services and they are likely to take several weeks, perhaps even months, if details are sketchy, so allow yourself plenty of time.

Baptismal certificates are more difficult to replace. If you do not have one check with your parents or, if that is not possible, ask the minister or priest what to do.

Marriage law in the UK applies to anyone marrying here, whether or not they are British citizens or domiciled foreign nationals or visitors on visas. However, foreign nationals may not marry by either the publishing of Banns (Anglican Church service) or on a Superintendent Registrar's Certificate alone. They must also apply for a Common Licence (for an Anglican Church ceremony) or a Superintendent Registrar's Licence with Certificate of No Impediment (for a civil ceremony).

Religious marriage ceremonies

Marrying in the Church of England

The Banns

Reading, or publishing, the Banns is the most common route to follow for a church wedding. It means that the minister reads aloud the names of couples who are planning to marry in his or her church and invites members of the congregation to register objections, should they have any. Only serious objections are accepted, for example, if there is a previous marriage which has not been dissolved by death or divorce, or there is a relationship within the forbidden degrees between the parties concerned. The Banns can be read anytime during the three months immediately preceding the wedding date. They will be read on three consecutive Sundays at the main service of the day.

> The tradition of the Banns had a real purpose in times when few people travelled far and most lived and died in the same community as their parents and grandparents. Sexual indiscretions in such circumstances could give rise to a real risk that courting couples may be closely related by blood without them actually knowing about it. Reading the Banns obliged anyone with knowledge of this kind to come forward and prevent what would be, in this example case, an incestuous relationship.

Once the Banns are read the wedding may go ahead on any day within the next three months but, if postponed for longer, they must be read again. In practical terms, it is unlikely that the minister will perform a wedding ceremony on a Sunday or other holy days since these are the busiest days of the church calendar.

Reading the Banns is not the only route to an Anglican Church wedding, although it is by far the most common. The alternative is to marry under a Superintendent Registrar's Certificate of No Impediment which is the civil equivalent. This is used for weddings in Catholic Churches, in other religious ceremonies and when one or both parties are foreign nationals. It is available, however, for Anglican services as well if reading the Banns is not a chosen option.

The minister will ask if you have both been baptized (christened) and confirmed. It is unlikely that you will be refused a church wedding if you have not, but expect the minister to want to spend more time with you if you are not church-goers. She or he will have to explain more to you and will want to be assured that you understand the nature of the preparations you are making and their long-term implications. You should also expect the minister to ask if you will be attending church services during the preparation period.

You will also be asked if you have been married before. The Anglican Church is still unwilling to allow second marriages in church, after there has been a divorce, although it does allow its ministers much more discretion nowadays. It is worth asking, if you really want a church wedding, and if you think your minister will be sympathetic to your circumstances. Even if a full church wedding is not possible, the minister may be happy to perform a ceremony of Blessing after the civil ceremony.

The Anglican Church is the established faith of the civil power in the United Kingdom which means that an Anglican minister is also a registrar. The minister supervises entry in the Register of Marriages directly after the service.

Marrying outside your parish

If the prospective bride and groom live in the same parish, arranging a church wedding is fairly straightforward but an increasingly mobile population is resulting in more couples planning to marry in parishes other than those in which they live. Most frequently, this happens when people leave the parental home, either to study or to work, and then wish to return there to marry.

If one of the parties lives in the parish where the wedding is to take place, and the other lives elsewhere, Banns must be read in both. The minister officiating in the parish where the wedding is *not* to take place completes a certificate saying that the Banns have been read there and the certificate is taken to the minister in the parish where it *will* take place. The couple is responsible for collecting the certificate and taking it to the officiating minister before the wedding day.

Both ministers will need to see all the relevant documents, that is birth or adoption papers, written permissions and death certificate(s) or divorce decree absolute(s), as appropriate, and both must agree to the arrangement. As before, anticipate that regular attendance at services may be expected in the respective parishes.

If neither of the couple lives in the parish where they wish to marry, at least one of them must establish residency there before approaching the minister to give notice of intent to marry. Attendance at one church service, at least, during this period will be expected as will attendance during at least one of the services at which the Banns are read. However, if the chosen parish is the family home of one or both of the couple, and their visits there have been frequent, including attendance at services, the minister may well use some discretion on the point of residency – it is worth asking.

Marrying in the Roman Catholic Church

Catholic wedding ceremonies are held under a Superintendent Registrar's Certificate of No Impediment and not after the reading of Banns. To comply with civil law, registration in the Register of Marriages is supervised, directly after the service, by registrars from the nearest district office.

The ceremony is held in a Catholic Church where the registrar will attend, to supervise the signing of the Register of Marriages after the service, in order to comply with civil law.

Marrying in the Religious Society of Friends (Quakers)

The Quaker faith does not have minister or priest roles in the same way as the Anglican and Catholic faiths. The congregation is administered in a democratic way so a Quaker couple will apply to the whole congregation, rather than to one minister-in-charge, to arrange their ceremony. This is done, normally, in writing to the Friends devotional service, which is called a meeting.

The religious service may be held in the Quaker Meeting Hall or anywhere else the couple and congregation chooses but there must also be a civil ceremony at the Registrar's Office or at another properly licensed place, in order to comply with civil law.

Marrying in the Jewish faith

As with other faiths, the religious ceremony of marriage performed according to Jewish rights can be held anywhere considered appropriate but a civil ceremony in a properly licensed place must also be performed if the marriage is to be lawful.

Jewish weddings are not normally held on the Sabbath (sunset on Friday to sunset on Saturday) or on certain holy days.

Marrying in other religious faiths

If the church, temple, mosque or meeting place is a registered place, a person licensed to register the marriage is present and a Superintendent Registrar's Certificate has been obtained (see page 19), then any religious marriage ceremony is acceptable in law. If the place is not licensed and/or there is no licensed person present, then a separate civil ceremony will be required before the marriage is legally valid.

Civil ceremonies

A civil ceremony may take place in either a register office, or at a licensed venue.

Licensed venues

Civil ceremonies used to be restricted to register offices. However, greater freedom now exists to hold a civil wedding ceremony at various venues throughout England and Wales. The venue has to be an approved premises (i.e. approved by the local authority); it must be a permanent structure, and must have public access. Many different licensed venues exist throughout the country ranging from stately homes, castles, hotels, permanently moored boats and even football grounds and zoos! The only thing they have in common is that they are all approved as being suitably solemn and reverent premises for the occasion. It is still not possible to hold legal ceremonies out of doors, in marquees or in private homes. An up-to-date list of licensed premises is available for a small fee from the Office of National Statistics, Local Services Office, Smedley Hydro, Trafalgar Road, Southport PR8 2HH. Alternatively, for licensed venues within your area, contact your local register office.

If you have a particular venue at which you would like to marry that is not licensed, you could approach the owner or manager to consider an application. The venue manager or owner would have to approach the local council, each of which has its own set of restrictions and application process. The venue would have to complete an application and provide the council with a copy of the plans of the building. The building is visited to ensure its suitability, access, fire precautions and other pre-set conditions. In some regions this could take several months, so if you would like to follow this route, allow plenty of time.

Legal aspects of a civil ceremony

Formal notice of intention to marry must be given in person to the superintendent registrar in the district in which you live. If you live in different districts, you must each go to your own district. If you intend to marry in the third district, you must also give them notice and provisionally book their time. It is worth bearing in mind that if you both live in different districts, and wish to marry in a third, you will be paying for three notices of marriage – one for each district.

At this stage you will also need to produce documentary evidence in the form of birth certificates or passports, and, if either has been married before, proof of how the marriage ended (such as a decree absolute). Once these formalities have been carried out, you are required to collect the authority to marry from your registration district and deliver it to the registrar who will attend your ceremony.

Notice of marriage can be given in two ways: by certificate or by licence. For marriage by certificate, both of you must have lived in a registration district in England for at least seven days immediately before giving notice at the register office. After this, you must wait for 21 days before the marriage can take place. The ceremony can then take place at any time within 12 months of the entry in the notice book. (You will have already used 21 days of the three-month period by the time you receive the certificate!)

Marriage by licence is often known as Special Licence. To be eligible for such a Licence one of you must have lived in a registration district of England or Wales for at least 15 days before giving notice. However, your partner need only have been resident, or physically in England or Wales, on the day notice is given. After notice is given, the ceremony may take place after one clear day (except a Sunday, Christmas Day or Good Friday). For example, you can give notice on a Monday, and get married on the Wednesday. Again, the Licence is valid for 12 months.

A civil ceremony must not contain any religious element, including hymns or other religious music. You can add favourite music, songs and readings without any religious reference, and you would still be able to use some of the popular bridal marches. An advance copy of any readings and songs that you would like to use should be given to your registrar so that they can be approved and included at the relevant points.

It should be noted that any music or readings to be used during the ceremony are often subject to copyright regulations. Check with the venue that you have chosen, to ensure that they have a licence to cover yourself against any breaches of copyright. Alternatively, you could contact the holder of the copyright direct.

Booking your venue and registrar

Many venues insist that you need to book the registrar before you book the venue; however, ideally, you need to book the venue at the same time as you arrange the attendance of the registrar or they may not both be available at the same time – a chicken and egg situation!

The best plan is to decide upon the venue first, and check the dates when the relevant room is available. Contact the registrar immediately over the telephone, with a few suggested dates and times, to secure a final date. All this can be done within a few minutes.

However, most registrars will take a provisional booking in advance, which will be necessary for the more popular venues that tend to get booked quickly.

Arrangements made for a marriage to take place at the licensed venue depend upon two things:

- that the superintendant registrar and the registrar for the district in which the premises is situated attend, and
- that the superintendant registrar to whom the Notice of Marriage was given has issued the authority for marriage.

Blessing services

If you wish to hold your wedding at a licensed venue, but would like a blessing, this must be done with a certain amount of discretion. Owing to the ruling that a civil wedding must be secular (non-religious), it is not possible to have any bible readings, etc. during the actual ceremony.

If you would like a religious element to your celebration, you could make arrangements with your venue to extend the ceremony beyond the attendance of the registrar. Contact your local vicar, who is likely to be very willing to attend the venue after the departure of the registrar for a separate blessing ceremony.

Alternatively, after a register office wedding, you could have a complete service of blessing either on the same or another day, to complete your wedding celebrations.

Other denominations

If you wish to be married according to a religious denomination other than the Church of England or the Catholic Church, you must obtain a licence from the superintendent registrar as described above. The building where the marriage is to take place must be registered for marriages, and the minister must be authorized to register the marriage.

Information about ceremonies relating to various faiths and beliefs is contained in Chapter 5.

Documentation required

When giving notice to the register office or informing the vicar of your intention to marry, you must provide:

- proof of your address
- proof of your single status if widowed or divorced
- proof of identity – for example, birth certificate or passport.

Licences and certificates

Certificate of No Impediment

Most marriages need only a Certificate of No Impediment before they can go ahead. If the wedding is to be held in an Anglican Church, the minister issues this certificate after the Banns have been read and, if the ceremony is a civil one, the registrar issues the Certificate after the List has been published at the register office.

Sometimes, however, circumstances are a bit less straightforward and then other measures might be needed, depending on whether the route is through church or civil means.

Common Licence

A Common Licence is the means of asking for permission to marry in the Anglican Church immediately after notice has been given and without waiting for the three-week period it takes to read the Banns. Application is made to the minister, in person, who submits a request to the Diocese Council giving the full circumstances of the applicant. Only one of the parties is required to give notice, but it must be made to the church in which the wedding will take place. For UK citizens resident here, there must be a good reason for the request, such as an imminent departure overseas, or the anticipated death of one of the parties.

A Common Licence must also be obtained by British citizens normally resident abroad but who wish to marry in the UK and by foreign nationals who wish to marry here.

The 15-day residency qualification *before* making the application still applies.

Superintendent Registrar's Licence

This has the same purpose in civil marriage as the Common Licence has in the Anglican Church in that it allows a civil ceremony to take place without waiting the usual 21 days after notice has been given. Reasons for applying for this licence are the same as for the church's Common Licence and the residency qualification also applies.

Only one application needs to be made, but it must be made to the Registrar's Office where the wedding will take place.

Special Licence

Application for a Special Licence must be made in person to the Faculty Office of the Archbishop of Canterbury. A local parish minister should be able to advise on procedure.

This licence allows applicants to bypass both the residency qualifications and the 21-day notice period, and it allows a minister to perform the ceremony in an unlicensed location. It is granted in few circumstances but these may include, for example, the terminal illness of one of the parties combined with their inability to leave hospital.

Registrar General's Licence

Introduced in 1970, this is the civil equivalent of the church's Special Licence. Circumstances and qualifications are the same and applications must be made to the registrar of the district in which the wedding will take place.

All these licences must be accompanied by a Certificate of No Impediment, which is applied for at the same time, and is valid for three months from the date of issue.

Second and subsequent marriages

In civil law, there is no ceiling on how many times a person may marry. Henry VIII had six wives, although most of us would find his method of ending some of his marriages a little extreme!

Civil law allows a person to remarry if they have been widowed or if a previous marriage has ended in divorce. Church law takes a different view. Both Anglican and Catholic Churches frown on divorce and remarriage, which is understandable when one considers the nature and solemnity of the vows exchanged during a church ceremony.

The Catholic Church does not recognize divorce which is a civil instrument for ending a marriage. Nevertheless, it does allow for annulment, which says that the marriage was not a true marriage from its beginning and is stricken from the record as though it had never been. Reasons must be good, and extremely strong – for example, if the couple married, being unaware that they were related within a forbidden degree. The process of gaining an annulment can take years and the effects are far reaching, for example, any children of the marriage are, technically, illegitimate.

Neither does the Catholic Church recognize civil marriage, since the ceremony conducted in a register office has no religious significance at all.

Members of the Catholic faith might, therefore, be able to marry again, in church, after an annulment or even after a divorce if the first marriage was a civil ceremony with no benefit from clergy.

Policy in the Anglican Church is broadly the same, although Anglican bishops and ministers are permitted some discretion to exercise their own consciences. Some are sympathetic to requests for second marriages in church, so it is worth asking the local minister for his or her views. Generally they will expect to see that both parties are committed to the church in a tangible way, for example, by attending services regularly and bringing up any children in the same manner. They will also expect to see that little, or no, fault can be attributed to the divorced party for the breakdown of the former marriage. Even then, the minister is still entitled to refuse to perform a church wedding, and is quite within his or her rights to do so.

An increasingly vocal body within the Church of England is pressuring the General Synod (the Church's governing authority) to clarify the situation formally. At present it is possible for divorcees to remarry in some parishes, where there may be a sympathetic minister, but in others, perhaps just a few miles away, that consent may be refused. An early solution seems unlikely but the pressure for change continues.

The law in Scotland

In Scottish law the minimum age of consent for marriage is 16 and, unlike in England, no parental consent is required for 16 to 18 year olds.

All notices of intent to marry must be made to the district registrar, in person, in the district in which the wedding will take place. Neither party needs to live in the district and only 15 days' notice is required. Since most weddings take place in spring and early summer, however, it is sensible to allow longer than the minimum notice period if you want to marry between April and July. If either party is divorced from a previous partner, at least six weeks' notice is necessary.

The registrar will need to see birth or adoption certificates and proof that any previous marriages have ended, such as divorce decree absolute or death certificate. In Scotland, the equivalent of a Certificate of No Impediment is called a Schedule of Marriage but in all other respects there are no differences. The registrar gives it to the couple to give to the minister in the case of a church wedding, or keeps it in the register office if the ceremony is to be held there or in another licensed venue. A civil ceremony must take place in a register office but a religious ceremony can be held anywhere, providing the minister agrees. In Scottish churches there is no reading of Banns.

Young couples eloped to marry in Scotland because the law was much less strict than in England. Gretna Green is the Scottish town closest to the border with England and it became famous as the first place over the border where young runaways could marry without the benefit of clergy or the need to seek parental consent (the age of consent in England and Wales was 21 at that time, but in Scotland, couples were able to marry without parental consent as long as they were 16 or over). Since then, the age of consent in England has been lowered to 18, so there are fewer runaways, but Gretna Green still acts as a magnet for some of the romantic young of England.

After the ceremony, the Schedule is completed with the signatures of two witnesses, both of whom must be 16 or over. The Schedule is kept by the registrar, if the wedding was a civil ceremony, or should be returned to him or her within three days if the ceremony was held in church. He or she then completes a copy of the Register Office Book of Marriages (the marriage certificate) for the newly-weds.

An English Superintendent Registrar's Certificate (of No Impediment) is valid in Scotland, providing the wedding is to be in Scotland and one of the parties lives, and has given notice, there. Alternatively, the party who lives in England can give notice directly to a Scottish district registrar by post, as long as the party living in Scotland has given notice in person. If notice is given in writing, at least six weeks should be allowed for formalities.

If a person living in Scotland plans to marry in England, Scottish registrars will issue, on request, a Certificate (of No Impediment) which is generally valid in England, even though certificates are not normally issued in Scotland. The party living in England should arrange for Banns to be read, or apply for a Superintendent Registrar's Certificate, as usual. However, the English minister is not obliged to accept the Scottish Certificate, and may request that the Scottish party fulfils English residency qualifications before accepting the couple's notice of intention.

The law in Northern Ireland

For marriages in Northern Ireland the procedures are almost exactly the same as those in England and Wales except in the case of a Superintendent Registrar's Certificate. In Northern Ireland, this is issued after only seven days, not 21 as in England. Every intended marriage must be notified to the District Registrar of Marriages, even if the ceremony is to be held in church.

An English Superintendent Registrar's Certificate is valid in Northern Ireland providing the wedding is to take place there, that one of the parties lives in Northern Ireland and that party has given notice of intent there.

A Superintendent Registrar's Certificate issued in Northern Ireland is valid in England for civil ceremonies and for ceremonies to be held in Nonconformist Churches, Quaker Meeting Places and Jewish Synagogues as long as one of the parties lives, and gives notice in, the district in which he or she lives in England. At the minister's discretion, it may also be accepted for an Anglican Church wedding in the parish where the English party lives, otherwise normal English residential qualifications must be met and the Banns read.

Marrying a citizen of a foreign country

Foreign nationals may marry here providing United Kingdom legal requirements are met. Only one of you needs to establish residency, however, which must be in the district where the marriage will take place, and only one notice of intent to the registrar or minister is needed. Nevertheless, the other party must be in the country on the day notice is given even if they do not actually live here.

If you are both foreign nationals, and intend to return to your country of origin, you should be sure that a marriage contracted in this country satisfies the laws of your own.

If you are a British citizen marrying a foreign national, and your prospective spouse has only temporary leave to live here, either to study, work, have medical treatment or for some other temporary purpose, marriage to you may not, necessarily, guarantee him or her permission to stay on permanently. A little extra planning might save much heartbreak later.

Marrying abroad

Going abroad to marry has become fashionable in recent years and several travel companies offer wedding and honeymoon packages to destinations all over the world.

Professional travel companies design their packages to take account of all the legal requirements both in the United Kingdom and in the destinations they recommend, as well as making them as appealing and romantic as possible. It is possible to arrange such trips as independent travellers, but careful checking with appropriate embassies or consulates at home, well in advance, is an absolute must and not for the inexperienced or faint-hearted.

The advantages are, however, easy to see; romantic places away from it all, a prearranged, fixed price and an escape from all the family pressures which sometimes threaten to hijack wedding plans at home, can seem very attractive when little sister insists on wearing Doc Marten's under her bridesmaid's dress and the flower girl develops hayfever!

Travel agents are best placed to advise on destinations. There are bound to be many more questions than is usual on a normal package holiday, so a pre-prepared list will come in handy.

The availability and popularity of these packages has grown enormously during the past few years and it is possible to travel to any one of dozens of different destinations all over the world. Still, some newly-weds find the experience not quite what they hoped or expected. Some say they felt 'processed' or 'packaged', which tarnished the romance a bit. The need to establish residency before the ceremony means that the honeymoon comes before the wedding, which some find a bit strange, unless you can afford to stay for three weeks (two weeks before and a week after the ceremony).

In Britain, there is no legal obligation for a married woman to adopt her husband's name so there is no need to change a passport or be concerned about your change of status when you re-enter the country – you can continue to travel on your old one. In some countries, however, it might be advisable to carry your marriage certificate with your passport just in case identity becomes an issue.

Planned Changes

Significant changes are planned during the next year or two – if time in the Government's legislative programme can be found. These will fundamentally alter many aspects of arranging a wedding. Notice periods, residency qualifications, the timing of ceremonies and the rules of licensing premises, among others, are all up for review. Outdoor weddings, not allowed under current legislation, might be possible, and the registrar (or 'presiding official') might be a kind of 'roving licensee' so that buildings themselves might not need a permanent licence. Consultations end in October 2003 so, if you are planning to marry in 2005 or later, check with the registrar, your local authority, minister, priest, imam, rabbi or other faith leader to see whether your plans are likely to be affected. They might not have much firm information for some considerable time after the closure of consultations but you could try the website of the Registrar General or the Office of National Statistics (ONS) for contact details and for Government papers, which will be published as they are released.

02

wedding etiquette

If planning a traditional wedding, you will encounter rules of etiquette that are steeped in history. There has traditionally been a 'right' and 'wrong' way to do things. Today, it is no longer necessary to stick to the set of rigid rules that have been developed over hundreds of years. Wedding etiquette today simply ensures considerate behaviour from the wedding party and guests, and gives you practical assistance in the dos and don'ts of the celebration.

Above all, when planning a wedding you should follow your own instincts, and do what is appropriate to the occasion. If you remember that everyone should be thanked, everyone considered, and no-one offended, you can't go far wrong.

Announcing the engagement

Speaking to your family

Once you have decided to marry, you may well feel that you would like the whole world to know! However, before doing this – speak to your families. It would be very upsetting to them to find out your plans via a third party.

Some men still feel that they would like to ask the bride's father for her hand in marriage, which is a nice touch of tradition. Sometimes couples announce their engagement together to their families. Whichever approach you decide to take, try to announce the forthcoming wedding personally, or, if distance is a problem, over the telephone. Try to speak to all parents within a relatively short space of time so that they are all aware of the news at roughly the same time.

Shortly after this announcement, you may like to get together with both sets of parents to discuss your plans, ideally over lunch or dinner when everyone will be relaxed and can get to know each other better. If you want something totally different to their expectations (such as a historical theme, or ceremony in a balloon!), you may wish to forewarn them so that they do not get any nasty surprises, and you do not have an argument on your hands! You may need to do some research prior to this meeting so that you can answer any queries posed to you.

Family dilemmas

Unfortunately not every couple has supportive families. Parents want their child to have a long and happy marriage and they might see a difference in religion, background, education, culture or age as a barrier to that hope. These parents might not receive news of an impending wedding with joy, and might even object very strongly. Some families are fractured by divorce and re-marriage, which can put a special strain on the bridal couple who see the spectre of argument, dissension and tension threaten what should be the culmination of their dream.

Most families will generally put such matters behind them, if only for the sake of the happy couple, if they possibly can. Some, however, will put pressure on their own child, or on the couple together, to abandon their plans and might even try emotional blackmail.

As long as you're sure of yourselves you will need to stand together and be firm. Ensure that your families don't succeed in driving a wedge between you and explain, confidently but calmly, that you've made up your minds and, whilst you hope they can be happy for you, their objections will not make you change your minds. Explain that you realize why they object, understand their concerns and have thought through how you will handle the issues your parents view as such serious problems. Be willing to listen to what they have to say, they have more experience of life than you and might have valid reasons for their objections. On the other hand, the problems they see in your future might be misconceived and you could do a lot to allay their fears if you are able to give them time, space and reassurance. Bring in a family friend, or someone you trust, to act as mediator if you think it might help.

Be prepared, however, that you might need to go-it-alone if you can't overcome their objections. You'll need to be sure that your marriage will be strong enough to cope with the knowledge that you've been the cause of fracturing your family, as well as with any real issues between you that your parents have correctly identified. It might be that they will come around in time, when they see that it's all working out well and that you're happy, but don't bank on it.

General announcement

After your parents, next you should speak or write to other close relatives and friends before any newspaper announcement is made. However, do not send out letters to everyone that you know, or despatch printed or engraved announcements – this could look like nothing more than a request for presents! Engagement gifts should not be expected, although your family may wish to give gifts in order to express their happiness and support for you. At this stage, if you have already decided, you will be able to ask those people that you have decided upon to act as attendants at your wedding.

Now you can tell the world! Conventionally, formal engagement notices are inserted into local or national newspapers by the bride-to-be's parents. The announcement may be worded according to circumstances, as shown below.

Formal announcement:

> Mr A Jones and Miss B Smith
>
> The engagement is announced between Adrian Jones, son of Mr and Mrs Benjamin Jones, of Ipswich, Suffolk, and Beverley, daughter of Mr Alan Smith, BSc, and Mrs Smith, of Norwich, Norfolk.

or:

> Mr A Jones and Miss B Smith
>
> The marriage has been arranged and will shortly take place between Mr Adrian Jones, son of Mr and Mrs Benjamin Jones of Ipswich, and Beverley, daughter of Mr Alan Smith BSc, and Mrs Smith, of Norwich, Norfolk.

Less formal:

> Mr A Jones and Miss B Smith
>
> The marriage will take place shortly between Mr Adrian Jones of Ipswich, Suffolk and Beverley Smith of Norwich, Norfolk.

or:

> Alan and Alice Smith are delighted to announce the engagement of their daughter, Beverley to Adrian, son of Mr and Mrs Benjamin Jones of Ipswich.

When referring to 'son/daughter', this normally refers to an only son or daughter; 'younger/elder' refers to the younger/elder of two; 'youngest/eldest' implies the youngest/eldest of three or more.

An announcement can also be made by the couple themselves, if they desire a more informal entry in the newspaper.

Informal newspaper entry:

> Beverley Smith and Adrian Jones
>
> Beverley and Adrian, together with their families, are delighted to announce their engagement.

The newspaper into which the announcement is inserted can advise on wording for other circumstances. However, for guidance the following wording can be used.

- If a father is dead, and the mother remarried after the death:

    ...., son/daughter of the late Mr Mark Brown, step-son/daughter of Mr John Graham ...

- If the mother was still married to the father at the time of his death:

    ...., son/daughter of the late Mr Mark Brown and Mrs Brown ...

- If the mother was already divorced at the time of the father's death:

    ...., son/daughter of the late Mr Mark Brown and Mrs Andrea Brown ...

- If the parents are divorced and the mother had remarried before the father died:

    ...., son/daughter of the late Mr Mark Brown and Mrs Andrea West ...

- When the bride has been married before:

    Mr and Mrs C Brown, announce the engagement of their daughter, Emily Jane Smith, to ...

If the bride's parents are deceased or are unable or unwilling to announce the engagement, the couple themselves or close relatives may do so.

A public announcement of an engagement should never be made if one of the couple is still legally married. However, if a previous marriage has come to a legal end, this does not affect the way in which an announcement is made.

One word of caution. Do not put your full address in any announcement as this could alert burglars to the existence of engagement and wedding presents on the premises. You will also find that heaps of junk mail from prospective suppliers will land on your doormat!

Engagement parties

If you intend to have a party to celebrate your engagement, the bride's family usually arranges this. It may be a large party for all friends and family, or a simple intimate lunch or barbecue in their garden for close relatives.

At some point during the gathering, the bride's father should make the 'official' announcement, giving a toast and welcoming the groom-to-be to the family.

Organizing your wedding – who does what?

The bride and bride's mother

Traditionally, the bride is queen for the day, having nothing more to do than say her vows, sign her name, throw her bouquet and look beautiful!

However, brides today are much more involved in the organization of their own wedding so that they get exactly what they want! This involves a lot of preparation, so the first thing to do is to obtain a lever arch file from a stationers, together with dividers that can be used to split up all the information that you will inevitably accumulate.

It is the responsibility of the bride together with her mother to:

- arrange for both sets of parents to meet
- discuss plans and payment with the groom and both sets of parents
- make a list of friends and family to be told, and arrange an engagement party
- together with the groom, select and appoint wedding attendants (bearing in mind their responsibilities)
- decide on the number of wedding guests to be invited
- draw up the guest list with the assistance of both sets of parents
- draw up the wedding gift list with the assistance of the groom

- draft a budget
- arrange wedding insurance
- decide upon the type of wedding wanted
- choose and book a venue for the ceremony and reception
- visit the registrar/minister and deal with the legal requirements
- choose and order the wedding cake
- write thank you letters for gifts as they arrive
- choose and book the photographer and videographer, transport, entertainment and flowers
- choose wedding attire for the bride and attendants
- choose, order and despatch stationery. Keep a list of the guests' responses as these arrive
- advise the best man of anyone specific to mention in his speech
- obtain gifts for attendants
- choose the groom's wedding ring
- wear in wedding shoes!
- arrange a display of wedding gifts
- arrange a rehearsal of the ceremony so that everyone knows what to expect
- enjoy the hen night!

The groom

The groom is responsible for the legal aspects of the wedding, choosing the best man and ushers, organizing the honeymoon, organizing clothing for the male members of the wedding party, buying the bride's wedding ring and a gift for the bride, and making a speech.

He should assist the bride with her arrangements as much as possible, but should also obtain the marriage licence, and, together with the bride, check all the legal aspects of the wedding. The documentation, ring and church fees are then passed to the best man.

The groom should arrange a honeymoon (increasingly, as a surprise to the bride), check that passports and any visas are valid, ensure that inoculations are arranged, and order travellers cheques and foreign currency as required.

The groom should ensure that luggage and going-away outfits are taken to the reception, and that a going-away car is available.

The groom asks his bride for the first dance of the evening.

The bride's father

He escorts the bride to the church, and the bride's mother-in-law in the recessional (going out of the church after the wedding). At the reception, the bride's father makes the first speech. Traditionally, he carries the burden of paying for the wedding.

Bridesmaids

The chief bridesmaid looks after the younger bridesmaids, and also assists the bride in her preparations on the big day. She holds the bride's bouquet as the couple undertake their marriage, carries emergency supplies for the bride, and may also act as a witness to the marriage. She also looks after the bride's wedding clothes when she changes.

The best man

The best man is usually a close friend – male or female – of the couple or the groom and is the 'organizer', handling details such as ensuring that the ushers are in the right place at the right time, and getting the groom dressed and to the church or civil venue in good time! He is responsible for organizing that transport is available as and when required, and for parking arrangements.

At the venue, he distributes buttonholes, corsages, order of service sheets and looks after the documentation and rings. He may also act as a witness to the marriage. At the reception he introduces the speeches, makes a speech himself, responds to the toast to the bridesmaids, reads messages to the couple, looks after any gifts received, and ensures that the car is ready when the couple wish to depart.

The best man also organizes the stag night, and, hopefully, prevents the groom from getting alcohol poisoning!

Traditionally, the best man dances with the chief bridesmaid for the first dance of the evening.

Ushers

The ushers seat people prior to the ceremony, and hand out order of service sheets. They may assist with parking arrangements.

The groom's parents

Traditionally the groom's parents have very little to do. However, in order to share the burden and cost of the wedding arrangements, they may offer to take on certain aspects of the arrangements, such as organizing and paying for the drinks at the wedding breakfast, or for an evening reception and entertainment.

Toastmaster

Hiring a toastmaster for weddings is becoming more and more popular. They relieve the best man of some of his responsibilities during the reception by formally announcing guests to the reception receiving line as they arrive, announcing speeches, proposing toasts and announcing the cutting of the cake.

Who pays for what?

Although it is traditional for the bride's family to pay, the cost of a large wedding today is usually shared. Many couples put some money towards the cost, and often the groom's family also contributes.

However, it may be helpful to know who traditionally pays for the various expenses.

The bride

She would normally pay for:

* the bridesmaids' dresses and gifts
* the groom's ring and gift
* the hen party.

The groom

He is normally responsible for:

* the wedding ring
* wedding clothes
* legal and church costs
* bouquets for the bride and bridesmaids, corsages for the mothers and buttonholes for the principal men
* presents for the best man and ushers

- the present for the bride
- the stag party
- transport to the church or civil venue for himself and the best man, and to the reception for himself and the bride
- the honeymoon.

The bride's father

He is responsible for:

- the wedding dress
- his own and the bride's mothers outfits for the day
- a wedding present for his daughter and her new husband
- press announcements, invitations, stationery and photographs and video
- flowers at the church or civil venue and reception
- transport to the church or civil venue for himself and the bride, the bride's mother and bridesmaids, and from the church or civil venue to the reception for himself and the bride's mother
- the reception
- the wedding cake
- insurance
- overnight accommodation for close family, unless they offer to pay for their own.

The best man

He is responsible for paying for his own wedding clothes.

Invitations

The style and wording of your invitations should reflect the style of wedding that you are having.

For very formal weddings, stationery engraved in script, printed on heavy folded card with the minimum of decoration will set the tone. Such stationery could include a reply card and return envelope.

For a more modern approach, there are many stationers that produce catalogues of invitations and other stationery. Invitations can be printed in a formal, informal, or modern style, and matching envelopes and even seals are available to complete the theme.

In order that there is no confusion, invitations should indicate whether the guest is being invited to the ceremony and wedding breakfast and evening reception, or just to the evening reception. Generally, invitations are worded as follows.

If the wedding is given by bride's parents the invitation should be as shown below.

Mr and Mrs Alan Smith

request the pleasure of your company/request the company of

....

at the marriage of their daughter

Beverley

to/with

Mr Adrian Jones

at St Mary's Church, Felixstowe

on Saturday, 17 June 20xx at 3.00 p.m.

and at a reception afterwards at

The Grand Hotel, Felixstowe.

(Reply address)   RSVP

If the wedding is to be hosted by both sets of parents, the invitation should commence as follows.

Mr and Mrs Alan Smith

and

Mr and Mrs B Jones

request the pleasure of your company

....

If the wedding is to be given by the bride and groom, the invitation should read as follows.

Beverley Smith and Adrian Jones

request the pleasure of your company/
request the company of

....

at their marriage

at ....

Invitations to a service of blessing

Invitations to a service of blessing following a civil ceremony should be worded as shown below.

Mr and Mrs Alan Smith

request the pleasure of your company

at a Service of Blessing

following the marriage of their daughter,

Beverley Smith

to

Mr Adrian Jones

at St Mary's Church, Felixstowe

on Saturday, 17 June 20xx at 3.00 p.m.

and at a reception afterwards at

The Grand Hotel, Felixstowe.

(Reply address)   RSVP

Civil ceremony – reception only invitations

With the ever-increasing number of civil ceremonies taking place in licensed venues, it may seem difficult to ask guests only to the reception. However, some licensed venues only have smaller rooms available for the actual ceremony, and thus the number of guests may need to be restricted.

In the case of register office weddings, the number will undoubtedly need to be limited, and thus not everyone will be able to attend the actual ceremony.

In such cases, the invitation wording should be as follows.

Mr and Mrs Alan Smith

request the pleasure of your company

at a Reception following the marriage of their daughter,

Beverley

to

Mr Adrian Jones

to be held on Saturday, 17 June 20xx at 4.00 p.m.

at The Grand Hotel, Felixstowe.

(Reply address)   RSVP

If necessary, you may like to include an explanatory note with the invitation, worded as follows.

Owing to the small size of the church/register office/service venue, only immediate family can be invited to the ceremony. We do hope that you will join us for the reception afterwards.

Wording for different circumstances

Here are various possible circumstances of those inviting guests to a wedding, with some suggested wording for invitations.

Wedding given by divorced parents	Mr Alan Smith and Mrs Alice Smith request the pleasure of .... at the marriage of their daughter, Beverley
Wedding given by divorced parents, where the mother has remarried	Mr Alan Smith and Mrs Alice Black request the pleasure of .... at the marriage of their daughter, Beverley Smith
Wedding given by bride's widowed and remarried mother	Mrs Herbert Robinson requests the pleasure of .... at the marriage of her daughter, Beverley Smith
Wedding given by bride's divorced mother and her new husband	Mr and Mrs Herbert Robinson request the pleasure of .... at the marriage of her daughter, Beverley Smith
Wedding given by bride's widowed/divorced father	Mr Alan Smith requests the pleasure of .... at the marriage of his daughter, Beverley Smith
Wedding given by bride's widowed/divorced father and new wife	Mr and Mrs Alan Smith request the pleasure of .... at the marriage of his daughter, Beverley Smith
Wedding given by bride's step-father	Mr Herbert Robinson requests the pleasure of .... at the marriage of his step-daughter, Beverley Smith
Wedding given by bride's foster parents	Mr and Mrs James Newton request the pleasure of .... at the marriage of their foster daughter, Beverley Smith

Wedding given by bride's godparent (and husband/wife)	(Mr and) Mrs James Newton requests the pleasure of .... at the marriage of her goddaughter Beverley Smith
Wedding given by others	Mr and Mrs James Newton request the pleasure of .... at the marriage of Beverley Smith, daughter of Mr and Mrs Alan Smith, to Adrian Jones ...

There are numerous variations to invitation wording, but hopefully this will give you a guide from which to start. Stationers will be able to assist with wording in difficult circumstances.

Alternative invitations

For an individual approach, you could make your own cards, or produce a design for printing by any good printer. Designs could include a photograph of the bride and groom, a black and white line-drawing of the church or venue in which the ceremony is to take place, a caricature of the couple or their pets/hobbies or any other relevant symbol – all of which can be printed onto invitations.

Sally and James are getting married!

Please row along and help us celebrate at the local beach hut known as The Grand Hotel, Felixstowe, Suffolk

at 3.00 p.m. on Saturday, 17 June 20xx

and afterwards for a reception under the tropical palm trees in the garden.

Note: Limbo dancing and fire eating not obligatory!

Dress: comfortable
Lei and grass skirts provided
if required!

RSVP 1 May 20XX
21 Golden Gate Road
Felixstowe, Suffolk

The wording that is printed could be much more relaxed than would normally be chosen. For example, if you wish your wedding to have a tropical theme at a civil venue with a reception in the garden afterwards and entertainment provided in the form of limbo dancing, fire eating and a steel band, you might word the invitation as on page 39.

This type of invitation indicates that the whole affair will be very relaxed, and that hats are not obligatory! Anyone wishing to wear their jeans, or even shorts, would not feel uncomfortable, and people will arrive dressed with a view to having a go at limbo dancing!

If you are to theme your wedding, consider ways in which the invitations may indicate this to guests. If you would like them to feel that they are able to take part in the theme as well, such as dressing the part in a themed wedding, indicate this on the invitation. If you do not wish this to be part of the invitation, write a small note to be included in the envelope giving them a rundown of your plans. This will mean that everyone has the chance to join in and not feel that they have missed out on something that they would have enjoyed.

The reception

Receiving line

If there is to be a formal receiving line, the function co-ordinator should be asked to keep the reception room closed until after the newly-weds, their parents and senior attendants, are ready to receive the guests. This may involve arranging for a member of the hotel staff to guide early guests into a lounge or waiting area for a time and offer them appropriate hospitality and refreshments.

The receiving line is made up of the bride's parents, the groom's parents, the newly-weds and their senior attendants, in that order, starting with the bride's mother closest to the entrance.

Receiving line

Guests →

Bride's mother	Bride's father	Groom's mother	Groom's father	Bride	Groom	Chief brides- maid	Best man

Top table seating plan

The top table accommodates the bridal party and there are several acceptable seating plans which cope with different situations. The first, and most common, is for nine people with the bride seated in the centre with the groom on her right, her mother on his right, then the groom's father and finally the chief bridesmaid/matron-of-honour. The bride's father sits on the bride's left and next to him sits the groom's mother, the best man and second bridesmaid.

Chief brides-maid	Groom's father	Bride's mother	Groom	Bride	Bride's father	Groom's mother	Best man	Second brides-maid

Sometimes this is not possible or practicable. Families can be extremely complicated nowadays, as divorce and remarriage/ partnership reforms them in new shapes, often leaving gaps and hostilities behind. It is up to the bride and groom to say what they want on *their* day since there is no right or wrong way of handling these potential problems. If it seems likely that tensions risk spoiling the day, hard decisions on who should be invited, or not, may need to be made early.

Complications might arise in families where both natural and step-parents are present, especially where there is some inter-relationship tension. A family conference several weeks prior to the wedding, if this is possible, may help ensure the wedding day is free from unnecessary difficulties and there are alternative seating plans which may also help to ensure things go smoothly. These alternatives should be discussed with the function co-ordinator when booking the reception.

Step-mother (Groom)	Step-father (Bride)	Chief brides-maid	Groom's father	Bride's mother	Groom	Bride	Bride's father	Groom's mother	Best man	Step-mother (Bride)	Step-father (Groom)

Best man	Step-mother (Groom)	Groom's father	Bride's mother	Groom	Bride	Bride's father	Groom's mother	Step-father (Groom)	Chief brides-maid

The alternative plans seat both step-parents and natural parents at the top table, while putting a little distance between them all.

Speeches

Speeches traditionally take place after the wedding breakfast. However, if the bride's father, groom or best man is particularly nervous about making his speech, it would be better to start with the speeches. They can join in, relax and enjoy themselves, knowing that the worst part is over!

It is usual for the bride's father to speak first, although tradition is changing – with the bride actually making the first speech nowadays in place of her father, particularly with couples being older when they marry, or when marrying for a second time. On occasion, another male member of the bride's family may be asked to make the first speech, such as an uncle or brother. He can then propose a toast to the bride and groom.

The groom will then reply, either on behalf of himself and the bride, or she may again step in at this point to say a few words. The groom then proposes a toast to the bridesmaids.

The best man then replies on behalf of the bridesmaids, gives his speech and reads any telegrams or other messages of good luck. He then announces the cutting of the cake.

There are several books on the market to assist with writing speeches. The speech needs to sound natural, and it is therefore important that some time is taken to practise what is to be said. As an *aide-mémoire*, cards may be produced with 'prompt' words written on them. However, if this course of action is taken, the cards should be joined with a string or tag to ensure that if they are dropped, they are not put back in the wrong order! Cards have the advantage of looking professional, and will not crumple or flap around like a piece of paper.

No speech should last more than ten minutes, as people will start to fidget if it takes any longer.

The bride's father's speech

Commence either formally, with 'Ladies and gentlemen' or with a more friendly tone, 'Friends and relatives'. As he and his wife are hosting the party, he will wish to thank everyone for attending, and say how nice it is to see everyone. He should then go on to talk about his daughter growing up – although he must *not* embarrass her!

The speech should conclude with a request that guests 'raise their glasses in a toast to the bride and groom'.

The groom/bride

The bride and groom are not expected to make long speeches. They should thank guests for travelling to celebrate their marriage, thank the bride's parents for hosting such a wonderful reception, thank the groom's parents for their support (at which point bouquets may be presented to both mothers), thank each other for marrying them and finally the bridesmaids for their assistance during the day. They should then propose a toast to the bridesmaids.

The best man

This is the hardest job of all as the best man not only has to bring a light-hearted touch to the occasion, but may also be acting as toastmaster, announcing the previous speakers and the cutting of the cake.

The best advice for any best man is to be sincere – and not to embarrass anyone present, particularly the bride, with vulgarities or risqué stories. Jokes at the expense of the groom are acceptable as long as they are in good taste! One-liners are often better than long, drawn-out jokes or funny stories. The best way to avoid embarrassment to anyone else is to make fun of yourself, your shyness or your inadequacy as a public speaker.

If all else fails, a professional speech writer can be employed to compose a speech. Make sure that it is written with your situation specifically in mind so that jokes do not fall flat or are inappropriate.

If nerves are a problem, the best man could commence by thanking the bride and groom on behalf of the bridesmaids, and then the cards and messages may be read out, before launching into amusing stories, etc. Finally, he should announce the cutting of the cake in order that anyone wishing to take photographs can prepare themselves with their camera.

Speeches are generally a very personal thing, and you should decide what you want. Ultimately, if you feel that speeches are unnecessary – don't have any!

Cutting the cake

The last part of the ceremony is cutting the cake. After the speeches the best man (or toastmaster, if there is one) announces that the bride and groom are to cut the cake. The couple leave their seats and, together, hold the knife over the cake and make the first symbolic cut, to the accompaniment of popping camera flashes and much congratulation. The cake is taken away to be cut into serving-sized pieces. If preferred, the cake may be cut before the meal. In this case, pieces of the cake may be distributed with coffee, while the guests are listening to the speeches.

While catering staff cut up the cake, guests leave their tables and will either move to another room, gather around the bar or, if this is a summer wedding and the facilities are available, go out on to a terrace or garden. As soon as the cake has been cut, waiting staff and/or the bridesmaids hand round pieces. Since the pieces will dry out if they are not eaten, only cut sufficient for those guests present.

If the cake is large enough, the top tier may be saved for later. Traditionally, it is earmarked for the first wedding anniversary or even the first christening. A well-made cake will keep for quite a long time, as long as it is properly stored. The icing may discolour a little over time, but it can be removed and replaced as long as the cake is still good.

> It is said that, if a bridesmaid sleeps with a piece of wedding cake under her pillows, she will dream of the man she will marry.

Gift displays

It is traditional to display your gifts at the bride's parents' home, as most people like to see the gifts that the couple have received. However, a display can be arranged at the reception in order that more people are able to view them, although this will not be as secure, and should be obscured from the view of any casual passer-by.

A table just inside the door at the reception will allow those guests bringing gifts with them to add them to the display. The chief bridesmaid or best man should take responsibility for the gifts and ensure that labels are re-attached once the gifts have been unwrapped.

Each gift on display should have the name tag attached. They should be arranged in groups of like items, e.g. all crockery together, all linens together, etc. Similar or identical gifts should be positioned apart in order to avoid embarrassment.

After the reception, the bride's mother should pack away all the gifts and store them safely until they can be delivered to the couple's home on their return from honeymoon.

After the wedding

After the reception, it is traditional for the bride to toss her bouquet. Today, bouquets are often pressed or freeze-dried and made into wonderful pictures to be kept as a keepsake. If the bride wishes to do both she could remove just a single flower from the bouquet to throw – or a few to preserve and toss the rest! Alternatively, she may wish to give her bouquet to a sick relative who was unable to attend, or, if either a parent, close relative or friend is deceased, to place the bouquet on their grave.

During the honeymoon, the best man/chief bridesmaid should return any hired clothing, and gather any receipts for expenses.

The bride's mother should send slices of cake to anyone unable to attend the ceremony.

On returning from honeymoon, the groom should reimburse the best man and chief bridesmaid for any out-of-pocket expenses. Any extra thankyous for gifts received at the reception, or not sent prior to the wedding, should be despatched as soon as possible. Notes should also be sent to anyone who sent telegrams, etc. It would also be a good idea at this point to entertain both sets of parents to a dinner in the couple's new home, to express thanks for the arrangements made.

Cancelling the engagement

Getting married is a huge commitment, and you will undoubtedly have some pre-wedding nerves. However, if the relationship really does come to an end, the most acceptable way of announcing the situation is to imply that the girl has broken the engagement. Formal announcements made to family and friends should be made tactfully and with discretion as there will undoubtedly be some disappointment.

Cancelling/postponing/modifying weddings

Hitches in wedding plans do happen; there may be a death in the family, illness or redundancy that leads to a change of circumstances.

If the invitations to the wedding have not been issued, only close family, the wedding party and friends need to know about the reasons behind the modification.

If, however, invitations have been sent, printed cards should be sent to inform guests of the cancellation or modification with wording as shown below.

Mr and Mrs Alan Smith announce
that the marriage of their daughter
Beverley
to
Mr Adrian Jones
will be postponed until 20XX
will not now take place

Or:

Mr and Mrs Alan Smith
announce that owing to the recent illness/sudden death
of Mrs Smith's father,
the wedding of their daughter
Beverley to Adrian Jones
at ....
on ....
has been postponed/will not take place.
The marriage will be held privately in the presence of the
immediate family at a date to be arranged.

Alternatively, if there is little time before the wedding was due to take place, a personal note or telephone call will suffice.

All suppliers of goods and services should also be advised, whether a deposit has been paid or not. However, any deposits that have been paid are unlikely to be refunded.

Any wedding gifts that have been received do not have to be returned in the case of postponement or modification to the wedding plans. However, if the wedding is cancelled entirely, they should be returned.

03

deciding what you want

This chapter is designed to help *you* with the decisions you will be making in the next few weeks and months. You will find that relatives and friends will all want to join in and even, sometimes, complete strangers will volunteer an opinion – have you ever watched what happens in a department store bridalwear section? People stop to stare and often cannot resist the temptation to pass a comment or two.

There will be constraints, of course, and most will be financial, but there will be the subtle (and occasionally not so subtle) pressure from family members as well as those of the clock and calendar.

From the day your engagement is announced until the day you walk down the aisle, or step into the register office, well-intentioned help and advice will come your way, whether you want it or not, so how can you ensure that you have the wedding day you want and still keep everyone else, including and especially your parents, happy?

In the following pages we explore the main decisions you need to make in the rough order of priority, with the plus and minus points of each option. There is also some indication of what you can expect to pay for the various options. You might find it useful to refer to the Countdown on page 170, while you read this section.

First, you should decide the time and the place, because almost everything else hinges around them.

Setting the date and time

Day and date

What should you consider when choosing the date of your wedding? Many couples choose a date which already has some significance for them, such as a birthday, or the anniversary of when they met. There is no reason, in law, why a wedding can't be held on any day of the year but you might find that you can't get hold of a registrar just when you want one; they're entitled to days off and holidays just like everyone else! Some faiths will also be very reluctant to arrange weddings on certain holy days, partly for reasons of tradition and partly because the place of worship and/or minister or priest will be too busy anyway.

The most popular day is, of course Saturday since it is the only day of the week when most people are not working *and* ministers/registrars are available. However, this is beginning to change as working patterns become more flexible and couples discover that some of the services they want on their wedding day are less expensive, or offer more choice, midweek. Providing the guests who are of most importance to the bride and groom can attend, a midweek wedding is something worth considering.

Summer months are the most popular, mainly because the weather is more likely to be good, because travelling is easier (for distant guests) and the photographs will look better. Warmer days also mean lighter clothing and less risk that special outfits will be ruined by rain or that the bride will need thermal underwear! Because the summer months are more popular they may also be more expensive – some providers of wedding services charge more in summer months. Some services, such as transport, may not even be available in winter. Many owners of beautiful, but fragile, vintage and veteran vehicles will not subject them to the ravages of British roads in winter, even for short journeys.

Even allowing for summer's advantages, the number of winter weddings is slowly increasing as people's holiday patterns change. More people now take winter breaks, which is changing attitudes towards taking time off from work in winter. It is more likely that preferred venues, and some other services, will be available at the right time because demand is lower. Hot houses ensure that florists can provide a wide choice of flowers, even in the coldest weather, and wedding gowns especially designed for winter are often stunning, using rich velvets in brilliant, jewel colours and 'fur' trims.

Time of day

To be valid in law, the exchange of vows and rings and signing the Marriage Register must happen between the hours of 8 a.m. and 6 p.m., Monday to Saturday, even if a religious ceremony starts before 8 a.m., continues after 6 p.m. or is held on a Sunday. The civil and religious elements can, however, be separated. It is uncommon for legalities to be separated in time and location from the religious aspects of Anglican or Catholic ceremonies but not so unusual in other faiths and religions.

This might change now that many more places are licensed for marriage ceremonies and couples ask for blessings, rather than full religious ceremonies in churches.

A civil ceremony in a register office, satisfying the law, can be completed in 15 minutes. A religious ceremony, however, can take place anytime, anywhere and last as long as necessary or desired. So, if you wish, you can have a religious ceremony on a mountain top at sunset on the summer soltice, but check with your officiating minister first! However, there are other considerations which will almost certainly affect the choice of time of day. For example, are guests travelling far? Will they be travelling on dark, wintery roads, which may take longer than at other times of year? Then there is the photographer, who will need about 30 minutes of daylight in which to take pictures. Events such as the local football team playing at home, or the town's street market, can affect traffic and although some events are not easy to predict, for example, whether there will be roadworks in the area, others often can be, with just a little forethought and planning.

The time of the wedding can also have an effect on the budget. For example, if the wedding takes place in the morning, and the reception is planned to go through into the evening, guests will need to be fed twice – lunch (the wedding breakfast) and, most likely, with an evening buffet. For a wedding in the afternoon, however, it would be acceptable to assume that guests had already had lunch before the ceremony and so cater for only one meal in late afternoon or early evening.

The duration of the reception may be affected by the newly-weds' departure plans, for example, if they are to leave for their honeymoon on the day of the wedding (many do not, arranging to travel a day or two later, especially if they have booked a package holiday abroad). If they are travelling, and need a few hours to reach their destination on the same day, they may prefer an early ceremony so that they can either enjoy at least part of the reception before they leave, or plan a shorter reception that will end with their departure.

As a rough guide, a marriage service in church generally takes between 40 minutes and an hour, depending on the length and number of hymns and the duration of the minister's address. If communion is included, an extra ten to 20 minutes should be added, more if it is a large congregation.

After the ceremony, the photographer will need about 30 minutes for photographs, sometimes a little longer if the families are large, or if some of the pictures are to be taken elsewhere, quite usual where churches are located on town or city streets and/or with little space for the photographer to work in.

After the photographs, everyone travels to the reception venue and guests are gradually greeted by their hosts and offered an aperitif and hors d'oeuvres.

Altogether, this amounts to somewhere around two-and-a-half hours from the time of the bride's arrival at the church until the time guests are being seated for the meal.

A civil ceremony is much simpler than a church service. If all the formalities have been concluded beforehand (payment of fees and so on) the whole thing can be concluded in around 15 minutes.

Register offices close at noon on Saturdays so the latest time for ceremonies to start will be 11.30–11.45 a.m.

Church or state?

Church

The image of a traditional, and romantic, white wedding in church is powerful for brides-to-be and for their parents. If both parties are practising members of the local Christian religious community, and neither has been married before, a Church wedding will probably be the first choice. Even those who are not regular churchgoers may still feel that marrying in church is the only proper way to do it.

If you would prefer a church wedding, first look in your local telephone directory *Yellow Pages* under 'Churches' and 'Places of Worship' and find the name of your local church. Call and ask to speak to the minister or priest, and explain that you would like to visit him or her with a view to discussing your wedding. The minister may ask you a number of questions over the telephone, or may just fix an appointment for you, reserving the questions until you meet. Both the bride and groom should go to this meeting.

If the wedding is six months or more in the future, this first meeting with the minister or priest may be a simple introduction, with a further meeting to sort out details, such as music, reading the Banns, and so on, planned for a little closer to the day, but it will ensure that the proposed wedding date is firmly in the church diary. The minister/priest will want to be reassured that the prospective bride and groom understand the implications and solemnity of what they are planning, and the Church's view of marriage and its responsibilities. Even the most liberal of clerics will take a dim view of his or her church cast in the role of simply a romantic setting for photographs.

If bride and groom live in different parishes both ministers/ priests must be visited. In the parish where Banns will be read but the wedding will not take place, a visit may be postponed until closer to the wedding date, around three months before is about right. The same paperwork will be needed, that is, birth certificate and so on, and many of the same questions will be asked in order to fulfil requirements.

The couple will probably be invited to participate in marriage preparation classes and encouraged to join the congregation, that is, attend services and take part in church life generally, if they don't already do so. A Catholic priest may ask about a non-Catholic partner's intentions for the future, to establish whether there is likely to be a conversion and whether any children will be raised in the faith. Each minister/priest is entitled to refuse to marry a couple if they have reason to believe that they are not committed to the Church's ideals of marriage.

The minister/priest will recommend a rehearsal for the ceremony at some stage, although probably not until very close to the wedding day itself. Both sets of parents, all the attendants and the bridal couple should be there so that they may practise their roles. This will help to calm nerves and ensure everyone is as comfortable as possible on the day itself.

Preparation classes

'Classes' is a bit of a misnomer really since preparations tend to be informal discussions. All churches view marriage as a life-long commitment which carries quite awesome responsibilities and every conscientious minister or priest will be committed to helping couples prepare for their new life together, not for his or her own sake, but for theirs.

Civil marriage

Many people have no religious belief or commitment and have no desire to be married in any church or faith. For those who have been divorced, and for those who have different faiths, a religious ceremony might be difficult, or impossible, to arrange anyway.

In order to be a legal marriage, only the civil part of a ceremony is necessary and there are a number of different ways in which this can be arranged. At its simplest, a marriage ceremony can be conducted at the offices of the local Registrar of Births, Marriages and Deaths in a specially designated Marriage Room. Registrars often go to considerable lengths to make sure the Marriage Room is welcoming and attractive. Most registrars will allow additional floral decorations to be brought in, poetry readings and the playing of taped music, if you ask in advance. However, as previously stated there must be no religious overtones, so gospel music, the presence of a priest or minister among the guests and/or the introduction of quasi-religious additions to the vows would not be allowed.

Most Marriage Rooms seat around 40–50 people, some more, and, whilst there is no aisle, there will be an avenue between guests' chairs which serves the same purpose, and a table with some flowers and so on as decoration, behind which the registrar will stand to conduct the ceremony.

Now that many more locations are licensed for civil ceremonies, however, there are many more choices of venue for a civil ceremony than ever before.

Almost every licensed place offers a complete wedding package, with catering, flowers, cake and so on, so there is no need to move to a different place for the reception or party after the ceremony. Costs are, inevitably, higher than those associated with a register office or religious venue because these are commercial concerns, with profits to make. Still, since some Ministers of Religion will perform a marriage blessing at these venues, thus combining the religious tradition with a new flexibility, the appeal is obvious.

Whilst not places of worship themselves, licensed premises do not carry the restrictions of a register office, where religious overtones are forbidden. In a licensed place, provided the registrar and the minister perform their respective ceremonies with a suitable separation between them, it is possible to combine a religious flavour with the civil ceremony, after a fashion.

Choosing the music, flowers and bells

Music for church ceremonies

Wedding music is triumphal, happy and often loud, providing an opportunity for the congregation to give full vent to the celebratory nature of the day. There are dozens of celebratory hymns and anthems suitable for weddings, and the minister/priest and organist will be happy to recommend some. Familiar words and music are best, since guests will be in much better voice with the tunes they know than with those they don't.

While guests wait for the bride to arrive, the organist will play a selection of musical pieces such as:

- A trumpet minuet by Hollins
- 'Nimrod' from Elgar's *Enigma Variations*
- Pieces from the *Water Music* by Handel
- The 'Grand March' from Verdi's *Aida*
- *The Arrival of the Queen of Sheba* by Handel
- The *Crown Imperial* by Walton
- Selections from Strauss waltzes.

As the bride walks up the aisle with her father, the organist may play:

- The first movement from *Sonata Number 3* by Mendelssohn
- The 'Wedding March' from Mozart's *Marriage of Figaro*
- The *Trumpet Voluntary* by Boyce
- *Fanfare* by Purcell
- *The Arrival of the Queen of Sheba* by Handel
- *March of the Prince of Denmark* by Clarke
- The 'Bridal March' from Wagner's *Lohengrin*.

There are normally three hymns sung during the service or, perhaps, two hymns and a psalm.

Popular choices are:

- Love Divine all Loves Excelling
- Lord of the Dance
- Praise my Soul, the King of Heaven
- For the Beauty of the Earth
- Now Thank We All, Our God
- All Things Bright and Beautiful
- All Creatures of Our God and King.

While the bride and groom are signing the Register, the organist and/or choir generally provide soft and gentle music for guests, or a soloist may sing. Examples are:

- *Air on a G string* by Bach
- *Ave Maria* by Schubert
- 'Minuet' from Handel's *Berenice*
- Theme from the *St Anthony's Chorale* by Brahms.

As the bride and groom leave the church together, followed by their guests, the organist will play a short piece which reflects the joy and excitement of the occasion such as:

- The *Pomp and Circumstance March* by Elgar
- 'Wedding March' from *A Midsummer Night's Dream* by Mendelssohn
- 'Toccata' from Widor's *Symphony Number 5*
- *Fanfare* by Whitlock
- *Bridal March* by Hollins.

It is a good idea to meet the organist in the church to talk over the selection of music, hearing how it actually sounds in the right setting. An organ played in church sounds very different from a piano at home, so sampling the real thing will be helpful.

The organist and choir leader should know each other and work together so, if the choir is to participate, they can be quite safely left to rehearse and plan together with the minister/priest once they know dates and the order of service.

The organ and choir are not, however, the only musical options available. Some churches have sophisticated sound systems and quite a few are regular venues for other sorts of music ranging from opera to rock to folk. Theatrical agents can provide solo singers, harpists, bands and musicians of all kinds and there may be local amateur performers, who are happy to play and sing at weddings. The minister/priest will often know who they are.

Secular music for use at civil ceremonies

The choice of music for civil ceremonies may include any of your own personal favourites, so long as they do not have any religious connection. This includes music that may not have originally been written with religious ceremonies in mind, but has been adopted for this purpose, such as the Wedding March from *A Midsummer Night's Dream* by Mendelssohn.

Other suggestions include the following pieces:

- Je veux vivre (from *Romeo and Juliet*) by Gounod
- pieces from *Carmen* by Bizet
- One fine day (*Madam Butterfly*) by Puccini
- Iche liebe dich by Grieg
- Bailero from *Songs of the Auvergne* by Canteloube
- Here in my heart (*Titanic* theme)
- The colour of my love
- Endless love
- You light up my life
- The wind beneath my wings
- Woman in love
- Eternal flame
- Everything I do, I do it for you
- Making whoopee
- Magic moments
- Love changes everything
- We've only just begun
- When I fall in love, it will be forever
- Music of the night
- I only have eyes for you.

Once you have made a decision on the music that you want during the ceremony, it is advisable to submit your selection to the registrar so that they can give their approval.

Flowers

Flower arrangements decorate many churches all year round, courtesy of volunteers from the parish. Through the centuries, groups of volunteers and patrons have been responsible for much of the church decoration we tend to take for granted today, things such as tapestries, hassocks, altar cloths and vestments.

Friends of the church will sometimes provide floral decorations for weddings, and often at a more modest cost than commercial florists. It is worth asking the minister/priest if this is a possibility, should the idea appeal.

Churches are often decorated more lavishly than usual at certain times of year, such as harvest festival. If the wedding date coincides, the wedding decorations will benefit without extra costs.

If a commercial florist is to provide all the flowers, she or he will need to visit the church before deciding what shape and size of decorations to recommend.

Bouquets for the bride and bridesmaids, corsages for the ladies and buttonholes for the gentlemen of the wedding party are usually paid for by the groom. However, the bride will wish to ensure that her flowers match those decorating the church and the reception, and may well organize the flowers as a whole.

When considering an alternative wedding, it is likely that flowers, or alternatives such as a parasol, a fan or a Bible, may be themed to match. Whatever you decide upon, make sure that it will be easy to carry. The bride will not want to have to use both hands to hold a bouquet, when she should be cuddling up to her new husband!

Flowers may also be used to provide beautiful headdresses. These are particularly suitable for period themes, such as a Medieval wedding, where a simple headdress of muslin adorned by a crown of ivy with a few miniature roses would be stunning. If the bride is striving for chic simplicity, a simple comb in her hair with fresh flowers attached and no veil is ideal.

Bridesmaids, particularly young ones, are often better off carrying a basket or hoop of flowers, a doll or teddy to match their costume or, in winter, a muff. Flowers look lovely, but the novelty soon wears off!

Bells

Last, but not least, there are the bells in church ceremonies. Campanology has many enthusiasts, although some churches do not have a group attached to them and still others have no bells, or just one that is used to ring the services. Here again the minister will be able to advise and a peal of bells, to complete the musical celebration in style, may be arranged if the circumstances are right.

Marrying outside the United Kingdom

Combining a wedding and honeymoon on some tropical, sun-drenched, romantic island, plus having someone else do all the hard work of organization, has an undeniable appeal to many, and particularly those who have large families who threaten to hijack the proceedings in their enthusiasm.

Travel agents offer an increasingly wide range of packages to places such as the Caribbean Islands, Mauritius, the Maldives, and so on. Travel and accommodation is arranged, as is the paperwork and formalities for the wedding. Travel agents advise as to what documents are needed, both before departure and at the destination.

Most of these trips are for about three weeks' duration, which allows a few days for any necessary residential qualification and for a honeymoon afterwards. Some hotels will move the newly-weds from their pre-wedding accommodation into honeymoon suites at the appropriate time and most packages include a post-ceremony celebration.

Although a three-week stay with all the trimmings can appear to be quite expensive, costs compare favourably with a small, simple wedding plus reception at home and considerably less than the average of around £16,000 for a traditional church wedding (2004 figures), excluding the honeymoon, in the United Kingdom.

Bearing in mind that the bridal couple still has to provide suitable outfits to wear, carrying them there and back in limited airline baggage allowances, and their friends and family are unlikely to be there to congratulate and celebrate, the foreign trip may suit only a portion of those planning a wedding. Most couples compensate for lack of family at the wedding by having a reception when they return home, although this can push up the final cost to what it would have been if they had married at home.

Reception

Planning the reception can be the biggest single task of wedding preparation. Many couples find themselves caught on a rollercoaster of providing a meal at a hotel (a buffet is not always an easier option!), wine, entertainment and so on and then a lavish evening party afterwards. Even when guests pay for their own drinks at an open bar, this arrangement can be very expensive – count on around £50 minimum per person for food and service, plus a facilities fee (for the hire of the room and basic decorations).

You may prefer something smaller, so what about a cocktail reception? After the ceremony, guests are invited to join the couple for a drink, a toast or two and canapés before the newly-weds take their leave after a couple of hours. It might take a little strength of character to stick to your guns when everyone else seems to expect a 'bit of a do' but, if that is what you want, then go for it!

Another way of minimizing the fuss, and avoiding the pressure to put on two separate functions, is to arrange the wedding ceremony for late in the afternoon (but remember it must be done by 6 p.m. to comply with the law) then host an informal party, perhaps with a light supper thrown in, afterwards rather than having a formal several-course dinner.

Yet another is to invite guests to join you at a public venue later, such as a nightclub, where you might pay all the entrance fees but nothing else. This could, perhaps, be combined with a small, intimate gathering for close friends and family immediately after the ceremony, where the traditional toasts and congratulations could be handled without breaking the bank on the cost front.

Most receptions are held in hotels, mainly because hotels provide the space, facilities and experience, and it is easier for those making the arrangements to leave it to 'experts'. Many of the places licensed for ceremonies will also host receptions, which has the advantage that you do not need to move anywhere, after the ceremony, except into an adjacent room.

Some couples put together their own receptions in a local hall, school or community centre. You will need to arrange for an alcohol and entertainment licence at the local Magistrate's Court, find a mobile bar, arrange your own entertainment and so on, which is hard work, especially if the wedding party is a large one, but it is less expensive and has the advantage of giving you more control over what you actually end up with. If the local hall is your choice, but you cannot face all the cooking, serving and clearing up afterwards, check the classified adverts in your local newspaper and *Yellow/Talking Page*s for mobile bars and caterers. They will supply kitchens, crockery, glasses and even the alcohol licence, if you need them to.

For something a little different, what about a river boat, a stately home, vineyard, theme park, fun fair or even Tower Bridge? All these facilities and places, and more, are available as reception venues (and even for the ceremony, if licensed). Check 'Wedding Services' in the *Yellow/Talking Pages*, with the National Trust and English Heritage, as well as advertisements in bridal magazines.

If the bride's home, or that of a relative or friend, is large enough, a reception can be held there, especially if there is also a garden to enjoy. If permission can be obtained from owners or managers there are also river banks, parks, woodlands and beaches. Marquees can be fitted out with beautiful linings, wooden floors, carpets, heating, furniture and kitchens so, theoretically, receptions and parties can be catered almost anywhere, even in inclement weather.

These options can be very expensive, however, since erecting a party-dressed marquee then taking it down again, including the day of the reception, can take several men five or six days. Then there is the cost of hiring all the furniture and equipment, not to mention the food, wine, etc.!

Whatever you decide to do, make enquiries well in advance to test the waters before you take the plunge as many venues and suppliers are booked solidly for months. Check, check and check again, asking for references from people who have used the service before and, if possible, using the facilities on offer as a customer before you make a commitment. Most locations will have an organizer, or co-ordinator, who will be able to give you information about what they can provide as well as the cost. Ask lots of questions, especially about what is included in packages – it is surprising what constitutes 'extras' (a cake stand and the knife, for instance) – since this is probably going to be the most expensive part of the whole day.

As an indication of cost expect to pay, in a three-star restaurant/ hotel: around £2.50–3 per head for reception drinks; £25–30 for a three-course meal; £15–20 for a buffet and £12+ for a bottle of wine. The facility fee for a stately home may start at £2,000 and rise to £10,000 or more (excluding catering, service and drinks) and to hire a marquee for 50–75 people can start at £1,500 (also excluding catering, etc.). On the other hand, hiring the local community centre might cost only £30–50 and a mobile bar might not cost you anything at all – the supplier may be happy with the profits from bar sales from your guests.

The menu

Sample menus, a wine list and prices should be included in the venue's information pack. A good hotel should offer choices of finger or fork buffet dishes, luncheon menus and full three- or five-course dinners with plenty of variety in hot or cold dishes, fish, meat and a good range of vegetarian/vegan alternatives. Check also whether the chef can cope with special diets, for example for diabetics, if appropriate. Most hotels will be happy to build a menu to a client's special request, if asked in advance, and will prepare favourite dishes, produce theme menus and cater specially for children.

Ask about drinks and bar facilities. It is traditional to offer guests a drink as they arrive – sherry, buck's fizz, a glass of wine or something similar, plus a choice of soft drinks for children and for those who don't take alcohol.

There should be wine with the meal, as well as mineral water and juices. Most restaurants will have their own selection from their cellar of white, red and rosé and will be happy to help you choose something appropriate, when you have decided on the menu.

If the budget will stand it, it is really nice to have something special for the toasts. Champagne is the favoured choice but it can be expensive and is not to everyone's taste. There are many excellent sparkling wines available which would probably suit most palates just as well and will add the same fizz and sparkle to the speeches and toasts.

Ask about bar opening times. Most hotel function rooms, restaurants and so on will have a bar licence until 11.00 p.m., and occasionally later, but do not take it for granted. If necessary, and with sufficient warning, a late licence can be obtained. The function co-ordinator should do this for you.

Special requirements

While discussing arrangements with the function co-ordinator, he or she should be advised of any other needs, such as access for a florist or party decorator (balloons and so on), or if any of the guests are on special diets or need help with wheelchairs. The co-ordinator will also want to know what entertainment has been arranged and whether access to put up equipment is required before the reception begins. Entertainers will also be grateful for a warning if the room has difficult acoustics which might distort sound: the co-ordinator should be able to advise.

Children, especially little ones, can quickly become tired and overexcited, or even bored, at adult functions so, if there will be children present at yours, you might like to consider hiring a clown or a puppet theatre to keep them entertained, or perhaps arrange for a video for them to watch.

Accommodation

Most hotels will, when arranging a wedding reception, offer rooms at special rates for overnight guests and might even have a bridal suite for newly-weds. If your reception is not at a hotel but you, and some or all of your guests, want to stay close by overnight make arrangements early to avoid disappointment, including booking the cabs to take you where you want to go. Check out local hotels and guest houses to make sure you can respond to requests for help from your guests.

Should a room be needed for children, to entertain or so they can nap, or if a room is needed for guests (so they can change and freshen up if they have travelled long distances) reservations for these should also be made in plenty of time to avoid disappointment.

Attendants

Whether or not you choose to have bridal attendants is up to you, although cost can be a deciding factor since it is traditional etiquette for the bride to pay for their outfits. Nowadays, however, bridesmaids often pay for their own.

Anything between one and six bridesmaids (or maids-of-honour) is quite usual. Female attendants are usually young, single females from the bride's family. If she has no relatives, or too few to fit the bill, then she will normally choose first from her fiancé's family and then from among close friends. A married attendant is called a matron-of-honour. There is normally only one matron-of-honour and she is always the senior attendant.

Girls under the age of six or so would not normally be expected to be a lone bridesmaid (children are quickly bored when expected to stand around doing nothing except look demure, which can account for quite a lot of time in a bridesmaid's day) and two attendants below this age would be sufficient. Every child attendant under ten should, ideally, be matched with an adult bridesmaid taking care of them while they are 'on duty'.

A flower girl, a pageboy and/or a ring bearer would normally be in addition to the bridesmaids, and adult attendants are expected to look after any little flower girls, pageboys and ring bearers, whose parents should be asked to help prepare them for their duties and make sure their poppets are happy to take part.

Male attendants are the best man and ushers, generally, but not always, in the same numbers as there are adult bridesmaids. Ushers are usually chosen from the among the young, single males of the groom's family. If there are too few male relatives that fit the profile, then some may be chosen from among the groom's circle of close friends and then from the bride's family.

Historically, the best man's role was to look after the groom in the days and weeks before the wedding to make sure that he did not change his mind, commit some misdemeanor (thereby disgracing his own and the bride's family) or get press ganged into the navy! Ushers were, and still are to some degree, guardians of etiquette on the day. They help the best man before the wedding, if needed, direct guests to their places in church, direct traffic and make sure high spirits do not spoil the celebrations afterwards, just as they have always done through the ages.

A fairly large wedding might have six bridesmaids (e.g. four adults and two children), a flower girl and a boy ring bearer, the best man and three ushers. The best man partners the senior bridesmaid in the procession out of the church and at the reception, and the other three adult bridesmaids are paired with the ushers, with all eight keeping a close eye on the four children.

Alternatively, the bride may choose to have just one attendant, say a matron-of-honour, who will pair with the best man for the procession and during the reception afterwards.

What to wear

Choosing what to wear can be a dizzy pleasure or a real nightmare! If you have started planning well in advance, however, don't worry too much about shapes and styles just yet although you might like to think about a colour theme. Consider the time of year you have chosen for the wedding, and what sort of flowers, fabrics and transport might be appropriate.

The bride's dress

The growth in popularity of the white bridal gown began in the mid-nineteenth century when Queen Victoria chose white, instead of the traditional royal silver, for her wedding gown when she married Prince Albert of Saxe-Coburg in 1840.

In ancient Rome the bridal colour was yellow. In Chinese societies, it has traditionally been red, highlighted with green and gold. This combination is thought to promote wealth, health and happiness.

Ready to wear

Shopping for the perfect dress is probably the most exciting part of wedding preliminaries, often involving the bride's mother and the bridesmaids as well as the bride herself. As with every other fashion, bridal gowns have their 'seasons', which begin with international shows in Harrogate and London during the autumn. Designs displayed there will fill the shops from October onwards, with originals selling for tens of thousands of pounds.

The range of styles and fabrics is immense, with colours from the palest of pale pastels, through ivory and cream to pure, shimmering white. Deep, jewel colours and tartans, heavy satins, velvets, brocades and many others may be added as trims or made into dress bodices, capes and jackets at any time of year or used for whole outfits for winter weddings, rather than the silks and taffetas traditionally used for summer brides. Ready-to-wear collections will start at prices from around £300, with made-to-measure and designer styles, especially those made with the more expensive fabrics, embroidery and beadwork, costing from a few hundred to many thousands of pounds.

Many retailers sell off their display stock in January and February and it is possible to find genuine bargains. They need searching out, however, because many bridal retailers don't advertise sales, and gowns with reduced prices are often displayed on rails alongside items still at full price. Most of the display stock offered at reduced prices will have been on the rails for a few weeks, or even months, but the retailer will almost certainly arrange for a dress to be cleaned for a customer, if it guarantees a sale. Bridal shops should also have an alterations capability, generally contracted out to home-based workers. Cleaning and alterations may be charged as extras, over and above the ticket price of the gown. Ask for prices before agreeing to a sale.

Hiring a dress

Wedding gowns can also be hired for the day. Most companies will hire out each wedding dress three or four times: the first hirer will pay around 50 to 60 per cent of the retail value, the second around 30 to 40 per cent and third and fourth about 25 per cent. Hire dresses are often sold at the end of the season, sometimes by the hire company direct and sometimes through dress agencies, which is a good way of acquiring a very expensive dress at a fraction of its original cost.

Dresses for hire are generally of simpler design and made of washable fabrics. Lace, beadwork and embroidery tends not to wash or dryclean very well so you might not be able to find as much variety in style or design from among hire ranges.

Alternative ideas

A traditional bridal gown may not be to everyone's taste and some designers specialize in making outfits that are just a little different. Retailers of evening wear often have suitable outfits, which may have more appeal for older brides, who may feel that traditional styles are a bit 'young' for them, or for those who feel that they would prefer something less elaborate for their second wedding.

To capture the romantic look and feel without the floor length formality there are ballerina and knee length dresses, in the same shades and fabrics as traditional gowns, plus pastel shades of peach, pink and blue.

For a slender figure, sheath styles are extremely flattering and for the bride with a sense of history, there are gowns which reflect the gracious age of Edwardian England or the roaring twenties.

Brides who prefer something a little more conservative might consider the larger bridal retailers who market ranges of suits, and dress and jacket outfits, often made from the same fabrics as bridal gowns.

Made to measure

Ready-to-wear bridal retailers do not, as a rule, hold stock; the dresses on display are for clients to try and then order which can take several weeks, or even months.

Similarly, dressmakers programme their time several months ahead, so early enquiries are essential. If the bride chooses to have an outfit made especially for her, it is important that she has a good relationship with the dressmaker. The dressmaker may be highly experienced and skilful but artistic interpretation on the bride's wishes will be so much easier if they communicate well and are on the same wavelength. It is helpful if you can take a photograph from a magazine, or a sketch you have made yourself, when you start to discuss what you want. Sometimes, especially if you are uncertain about what you want, it is a good idea to try some styles on in a shop first, even if you are planning to have your dress made.

For shopping trips, the companionship of someone whose judgement the bride trusts is invaluable. The final selection belongs, of course, to the bride, but a helping hand and another pair of eyes when reviewing the huge selection of dresses on offer will generally be more than welcome. You may find that you need to try on many before deciding what really suits you and fits in with the style of wedding you're planning.

Accessories
There are many more accessories to choose from than there are dresses so it is sensible to go for the dress first and then search for the right accessories. Shoes can be dyed to match outfits and headdresses can always be made to order.

Larger bridal wear retailers generally stock a whole range of accessories from veils to garters and headdresses to shoes. Shoes should feel comfortable right from the start since the bride is likely to spend most of the wedding day on her feet. Wearing them indoors at every opportunity will break them in before the big day.

Buying
Bear in mind that you may be buying an outfit in February to wear in August, or perhaps the other way around – the weather will be very different when you wear it for real.

Whether the choice is for ready made, hire or made to measure, bridal magazines are the best place to start looking. Every issue contains dozens, sometimes hundreds, of designs, plus information on stockists. *Yellow Pages* is a good source of information for local areas: check 'Ladies Wear, Hire', 'Dressmakers', and 'Wedding Services'.

Having decided what you want, the best time for shopping is around five to six months before the wedding. Too early and there is a risk that something better will come along after the budget has been spent, and a free choice may not be possible. If the dream dress proves to be somewhat illusive in the retail sector, there is still time, at around four to five months before the wedding, to have a dress made.

Going-away outfits

Most newly-weds want to stay and enjoy their reception and the party which almost always follows well into the evening. Few, nowadays, leave half-way through the proceedings to travel somewhere else to spend their honeymoon night.

Traditionally, however, newly-weds who were wealthy enough to have a honeymoon changed out of their wedding clothes into something more appropriate for travelling and left their guests to enjoy the rest of the party. Nowadays, fewer couples leave the reception this way – many go on their honeymoon a few days later (largely because holiday charter flights take advantage of off-peak reductions in airport tariffs) or simply stay on at the reception in order to enjoy themselves alongside their guests. If this is the case, the bride will often stay in her wedding dress as long as possible – and who would blame her – changing into a party or cocktail outfit later in the evening. Buying a wedding dress, a party outfit *and* something to go away in later can work out to be quite expensive but there are few reasons as good as one's wedding day for a little self-indulgence!

If the groom is married in a lounge suit, he may feel it will double as his going-away suit as well, but if he has married in a morning suit, a uniform or highland dress, he, too, may splash out on something new for his honeymoon.

Bridesmaids and the matron-of-honour

Bridesmaids are most often dressed in a style and colour that complements the bridal gown. When the bridesmaids are all of similar colouring, age and build this works very well but if not, one alternative is to choose a common style but different colours. This works best when there are several bridesmaids, for example, one pair might wear pale blue, another lavender, and so on.

The bride and her attendants should all be in agreement, which may need a bit of give and take. A red-head, for example, may have very strong opinions on wearing the bride's favourite baby pink, and the elegant Edwardian style she favours may not suit the six year old as well as the 26 year old.

The superstitious may wish to avoid any shade of green, even turquoise, since it is said to be unlucky at a wedding.

As with the bridal gown, the dresses may be bought at a ready-to-wear shop, hired for the day or made to measure. Etiquette says that if a dress is suitable for alternative wear, as a ballgown, for example, the bridesmaid should pay for her own dress and keep it after the wedding. If, however, a dress is clearly unsuitable for wearing again, the bride (or her father, if he is the host in a full, traditional, sense) pays and the dress is the bridesmaid's to keep or dispose of.

To hire a bridesmaid's dress costs from £45 upwards, with made-to-measure and ready-to-wear dresses from around £65. Designer dresses and/or those made from more expensive fabrics can cost quite a bit more.

Hire companies generally carry a wide range of colours although not, necessarily, a wide choice of styles. Dresses should be cleaned or laundered between each hiring, so check necklines, hems, wrists and under arms for tell-tale signs.

Timescales for searching and shopping are about the same as for the bridal gown, but it is prudent to choose the bridal gown before shopping for bridesmaids' outfits.

Children

Small bridesmaids often wear the same style and colour of dress as the adult attendants but, if the adult style is unsuitable for children, dressing them differently is quite acceptable as long as the different outfits complement each other in some way. As with adult styles, little dresses can be bought at ready-to-wear retailers, hired for the day, or made to measure. Prices for hiring start at around £30, and expect to pay from £40 upwards to buy either ready to wear or made to measure. Designer dresses can easily cost several hundreds of pounds, even for small children's dresses.

For pageboys and ring bearers, hiring an outfit is by far the best option. Small versions of highland dress, costumes of satin shirts and knee breeches and miniature morning suits are available from menswear hire shops and prices start from around £30.

The main consideration, when choosing outfits for child attendants, is that they will almost certainly wear them for a good part of the day, perhaps from quite early in the morning until the reception ends or they are taken home to bed. Children can be tough on clothes, so hiring may not be the best option since any damage will be charged to the customer. However, if the bride has set her heart on a miniature morning suit, or a Cinderella-style footman's satin suit, the solution may be for children to change out of their hired outfits immediately after the ceremony and before the reception actually begins.

Menswear

What the men wear depends, to a great degree, on the style of wedding. Nowadays many men live and work in casual clothes and some marry in them as well although it is not very common, even in today's relaxed society. Lounge suits are quite acceptable and will repay the investment by being wearable on other occasions.

Morning suits are increasingly popular, with many good menswear shops having a hire section. To hire a complete outfit of trousers, tail coat, cravat, gloves and hat will cost from about £70 upwards, depending on size and quality. Remember that it is usual for the groom, ushers, and best man to wear the same colours and style, except, perhaps, for the cravat and optional waistcoat, where differences can lend a touch of originality to an otherwise uniform look.

Most menswear for weddings is hired for the occasion nowadays. Since the hire market is quite substantial and widespread, most towns have at least one gentlemen's outfitters that will hold, or have access to, a range of items. Once again, *Yellow Pages* will help to locate them.

Reputable companies will clean a suit each time it is hired but, to be sure, check pockets, turn-ups and under the collar for confetti – if it is there, the chances are that the suit has not been cleaned since it was last worn.

The groom and his attendants should, wherever possible, arrange to hire their suits from the same outfitters, or the same branch if the outfitter is one of a chain or franchise. Different shops stock the work of different tailors, and the shades, colours and styles vary from place to place, even within the same company. Fittings should be arranged, and reservations made, around three months before the wedding.

Alternatives

Members of the armed forces are permitted to wear uniform for their weddings, although few women take up the option for obvious reasons.

During the Second World War many brides wore their uniforms, partly because the rationing of fabrics and clothes allowed little choice and partly because, under the pressures of operational requirements, many marriages were arranged very quickly.

Servicemen, on the other hand, do marry in uniform, often at the request of the prospective bride and both sets of parents. Dress uniforms are out of the ordinary, frequently spectacular to look at, and look wonderful in the photographs. They also have a distinct advantage in that they involve little, or no, extra expenditure!

If the groom is in the services, it is likely that some of the guests and the best man may also be in the services. If so, they would generally be expected to wear uniform. It may even be possible, if they are in the appropriate services and ranks, to arrange a guard of honour, with an archway of drawn swords under which the procession out of the church would pass.

If the groom is a Scot, he may wish to wear full, ceremonial dress in his clan tartan. These can also be hired for the day, although, generally, hire companies supply only the most common tartans. Clan tartans can be bought ready made or to order. There are more companies providing this service in Scotland than in other parts of the United Kingdom, but most will work by mail order, if required.

Going abroad

If you are planning a beach wedding, or a ceremony somewhere other than at home in the UK (especially if air travel is involved), the traditional sort of wedding dress may not be very suitable, simply because of the difficulties of taking it with you on the journey. They can take up a great deal of space and are actually quite heavy. Still, some fabrics travel well, and can be packed in very small spaces without crushing, so it is worth asking a wedding specialist dressmaker what is available.

Some package companies supply a selection of outfits to hire at the destination, although there may not be much choice and each may very well have been worn by several brides or grooms before you. Feedback from some couples says that these outfits are not always clean and may even be damaged.

If your ceremony abroad is to be held on a beach or by a pool in hot, strong sunlight, the type of outfit you will be looking at in the UK may not be especially appropriate anyway, so why not consider something much more relaxed, such as a shalwar kameez or sarong style.

Transport

'Just get me to the church on time', says the song, and it's true that transport is what brings everything together on the big day.

A car is the most common form of transport hired for a wedding, but there are many different sorts of car and a wide variety of other forms of transport to choose from. Most families have access to several cars nowadays and hiring vehicles may not be necessary. They can be very expensive to hire anyway, starting at around £350 just for one vehicle, such as an older style Bentley and driver, up to £1,000 or more for horse and carriage.

If you are considering using your own vehicles, or borrowing something from a friend or colleague, think ahead to who is going to drive (key figures may need to be somewhere else – in the church, for example!) and how the vehicles are to be decorated for the day. Prices vary a great deal, generally because providers range from the enthusiastic owner/driver, who wants to earn enough to pay for the upkeep of his pride and joy, to nationwide vehicle hire companies.

A white Rolls Royce is always popular, and Rolls Royce and Bentley limousines are probably the most commonly hired wedding cars but you can have a 1950s' Cadillac, a Model T Ford, a Routemaster double decker bus or just about any other sort of vehicle, if you like. Just look under 'Vehicle Hire' or 'Wedding Services' in your local *Yellow Pages*.

Vintage and veteran cars and horse-drawn carriages are the next most popular, but brides have been taken to the church or register office in motorcycle sidecars, helicopters, boats and every conceivable type of transport there is.

Local papers have advertisements for wedding cars for hire and more can be found in your *Yellow Pages*. If the choice is for a specialist vehicle, such as a vintage Rolls Royce or 'Cinderella's magic coach', it is important to book early because there are not many of them around and it is a case of first come, first served.

Many vintage and veteran cars are small inside, something to remember if the wedding dress has petticoats, hoops and/or a train. They are more expensive simply because they tend to be fragile and require expensive maintenance and insurance cover to keep them on the road. Many owners will not accept bookings for the winter months, because of the strong possibility of inclement weather. Remember that the bride's hair and veil, at least, will be affected by a trip in an open-topped tourer.

Before the ceremony

The bride's transport

The bride's transport is very important, not just because it brings her to the church or civil venue but because the whole day hinges around it being at the right place at the right time. At certain times of year the church may have more than one wedding booked during the day, and a register office is likely to have several, so a late arrival could threaten the arrangements of more than one family.

Before booking the transport and confirming with a deposit, take a little time to visit the owner, or company, and view the vehicle. Whether the vehicle belongs to a large company or an owner driver, they should be happy to arrange a viewing and may even be able to arrange for the car to be seen 'dressed' ready for a wedding, if asked.

Things to check, before making a booking, are:

- will the car be used for weddings other than yours on the day? There could be a knock-on effect of delays earlier in the day, or you may have to sit on someone else's confetti!
- what are the arrangements for an acceptable substitute, should the car break down (preventing it from arriving on time or completing the job) or be sold before the wedding date?
- will the flowers in the car be fresh (unless silk or parchment are preferred)? Bear in mind that fresh flowers may be charged as an extra.
- will ribbons be new (i.e. not used before)?
- will an umbrella be available, in case it rains (golf umbrellas are ideal, since they have a generous spread of protection)?

You should also ask for the vehicle to arrive at least half an hour before it is due to leave the bride's house for the church. (This is a precaution against unexpected delays. Even if the vehicle is 10 to 15 minutes late, the time lost will be absorbed by the half-hour 'cushion' and the ceremony will not be delayed.)

The bridal party

A second car may seem like a luxury, when thinking ahead some six months or so but, on the day itself, it becomes a real boon and, in some cases, an absolute necessity. For a church wedding, the second vehicle will take the bride's mother and the bride's attendants to the church.

If the party is moderately large, say four bridesmaids, the bride's mother and a pageboy, an ordinary saloon will not be large enough to transport them all together. The driver may be willing to make two trips from the house to the church or civil venue but this takes time, 20 to 30 minutes for even the most modest round trip, which may be just too long. Alternatively, a stretched limousine might be the answer. Some extra long vehicles carry seven or eight people in comfort, necessitating only one trip for the whole group.

For a register office ceremony, the bride and her father will need transport and, if the wedding is small, the bride's mother may find herself travelling to the ceremony alone. To provide a second car for one person may not be a necessity, but it would almost certainly be welcome. It could be shared with the bride's siblings or the groom's parents and would be most useful after the ceremony, taking family to the reception.

After the ceremony

To the reception

After the ceremony the vehicle that took the bride and her father, or other escort, to the church or register office, will now take the newly-weds to the reception. Sometimes this car will return to the church or register office and pick up the bride's parents, in the absence of a second vehicle being available, but this will delay the reception because the receiving line will not be complete until all four are together with the groom's parents, the best man and the chief bridesmaid or matron-of-honour.

Attendants will also need transport to the reception and, in the absence of a second hired car, family members and guests will need to be pressed into service as unpaid 'taxi' drivers for those who find themselves without wheels at critical moments.

However it is arranged, the essentials are that the newly-weds, the bride's parents, the best man, chief bridesmaid or matron-of-honour and groom's parents (if they are to join the receiving line, which is a matter of choice) should arrive at the reception venue as quickly as possible after the ceremony has been completed.

During the reception

During the reception transport will be needed for any number of reasons. Parents with small children need to take them home, Aunt Nell needs to get to the station for the last train and the groom's brother needs to go home to change because little Billy was sick over his suit – they all may be unable to drive because they are over the limit or there may be a 30-minute wait for a taxi.

A car on call during the reception may not be absolutely necessary, but it can be a blessing as the day and evening pass.

Going away/coming home

Many honeymooners travelling to destinations abroad spend a night or two either at their own home, or at a hotel, after the ceremony and before their flight. Either way, some form of transport is needed to travel to the honeymoon hotel or to the airport/port of embarkation.

Most couples will undertake this journey under their own steam, but the company which supplied the bridal car (providing it was a car, of course, and not a horse-drawn carriage) will arrange for the same vehicle to take the newly-weds to their honeymoon hotel, or to their air or ship departure point, and collect them at the end of their honeymoon. It saves on expensive airport parking and ensures that the atmosphere of the occasion is prolonged for as long as possible.

Horse-drawn vehicles are slower than cars, so journeys which may take a few minutes by car are likely to take much longer in a carriage. Unless the horse(s) are stabled very close to the bride's home, both horse(s) and carriage will be ferried in trailers to a convenient location nearby, such as a car park, where they can be offloaded, tacked-up and dressed. The procedure is reversed when the job is finished and the whole process, including the wedding itself, is likely to take two people five or six hours, plus travelling time from their base, which is why carriages are more costly to hire than cars.

Photography and video recording

Finding a photographer is relatively easy, finding a good one, who understands wedding photography, needs a bit more investigation. Good photographers tend to be booked for some time in advance so you should consider booking around five to six months before the wedding, or even a little earlier. Any photographer should be willing, and able, to show you examples of previous commissions, explain how he or she works and what he or she will do on the day, and afterwards. Most work to a tried and tested formula, with a few extras available on request. The photographer should be at the church or civil venue before the first guests arrive and will take a few shots before the ceremony, generally of the key players, such as the groom and his best man, and the bridesmaids, as they arrive. He or she will photograph the arrival of the bride and her father and, if the minister or registrar permits, as they walk up the aisle. The photographer should also be willing to visit the bride's home before she leaves for the ceremony (to take some pictures in the garden, for example) and to go with the bridal party to a location away from the church for pictures if the church or register office is not photogenic or has insufficient space for pictures. An extra charge may be made for these additional services.

A basic photography package will include:

- a visit to the wedding location to assess the best picture potential
- a visit to the bride's home and reception venue (if pictures are to be taken there)
- between 40 and 100 'proof' shots from which the couple make a final selection
- an album (different qualities will be available)
- the chance for relatives/friends to buy copies (at extra cost)
- reprint potential for a specified period of time after the wedding (at extra cost)
- insurance.

One of the most moving moments of the whole day, generally caught by only the quickest of cameras, is the groom's face as he turns to watch his bride walking up the aisle towards him.

Extras may include visiting the church or civil venue prior to the wedding day to take shots while the building is quiet, and going on to the reception to take pictures of the receiving line, speeches and cutting the cake. There should also be a choice of album, covering a range of cost options. The more experienced the photographer and the more pictures taken, the higher the charges will be. Costs of around £550 to £600 are about average but £1,000 or more is by no means unusual.

The proof photographs are for circulating among friends and relatives so that they may choose examples they wish to keep, which are then ordered from the photographer. Copyright belongs to the photographer and pictures may not be copied without consent. Although, technically, copy pictures can be made from prints, any reputable processing laboratory or photographer, other than the one who took the original pictures, will refuse to do so, since this kind of copying breaks copyright law. If your family is large, or the proofs need to be sent abroad, it is worth asking for two sets of proof prints. The photographer usually keeps negatives for up to two years, but check in order to avoid disappointment later.

Video recording is becoming increasingly popular providing, as it does, a more vibrant record of the day than is possible with photographs alone. As with the photographer, ask to see examples of work before deciding and ask how the recording will actually be made. The best wedding videos come from two (or more) cameras, strategically placed to capture different aspects of the same course of events, edited together afterwards for presentation.

Cameras are generally static, in order to be as unobtrusive as possible to the ceremony and guests. In most cases two cameras is the optimum, since three or more tend to pick each other up, in shot, too often. Editing, and the addition of music and titles, should be included in the price and some companies will add a commentary to the finished product, if asked, as an extra.

The video camera operator will work to a schedule similar to that of the photographer, and they should meet and confer before the day itself to ensure they can work together.

The cost of videoing a wedding varies a great deal around the country and price is not always a good guide to quality. Expect to pay anything from £200 to £1,000, depending on the experience and reputation of the company, location and extras.

Some ministers and priests will not permit photography or videoing inside the church; check first to avoid last-minute disappointments.

Flowers

Most florists provide wedding flowers. More than the cake and the reception venue, flowers are a very personal thing for the bride, second only to her choice of dress. With hot houses providing extended flowering seasons almost everywhere, all kinds of flowers are available all year round. Roses at Christmas may be a little more costly, but they are there for the bride who wants them.

Florists will advise on availability, and designs are generally chosen from illustrated catalogues, or the bride may provide a picture of a special design. The most commonly placed order is for a bridal bouquet, sprays for the bride's mother and bridesmaids and buttonholes for the groom, the best man, the bride's father and the ushers. Extras may include pedestal displays for the chancel steps at the church, for the reception venue or for the register office, decorations for the ends of pews and around entrances and exits, an arch under which the newly-weds may have pictures taken, sprays and garlands to decorate the top table at the reception, headdresses for the bride and her attendants and fresh flowers in the bridal car.

Visit the florist of your choice well in advance, and put your wedding date in the diary, but a final choice of which flowers you want can wait until around three to four weeks before the date, if you prefer to wait that long. By this time the florist will have a better idea of what is available and the cost, since this can vary quite a bit now that flowers travel half-way across the world.

Flowers are usually delivered on the day they are used or, if they are needed very early, late on the day before. Bearing in mind that buttonholes for the men may be part of the order, and the best man may need the ushers' buttonholes quite early, flowers should be delivered/collected in plenty of time.

To keep flowers fresh, spray them liberally with cool, fresh water (preferably distilled, if the local tap water is very hard, since hard water leaves unsightly lime or chalky deposits as it dries) and store them in a cold place or in a refrigerator set at 1 or 2.

If the florist can also see a picture of the dress, she or he will probably make helpful suggestions as to size, design and colour of the bride's flowers, taking into account that the flowers should enhance the whole picture, not overshadow either the dress or the bride.

Most pedestal arrangements are made of two or more pieces fitted together, usually the top bowl, in which flowers are arranged, and the stem of the stand. They are quite heavy, and the flowers themselves are fairly fragile but, with care, they can be transferred from one place to another. This means that flowers used in a church or register office could be moved to the reception while the photographic session is underway, providing there are two or three strong pairs of arms to take care of it. If in doubt, have a word with the florist when placing the orders.

It is occasionally possible to share the expense of these larger displays if there is another wedding on the same day. The minister/priest/registrar may be willing to put the brides in touch with one another, if asked, to see if it could be arranged.

Fresh flowers are always the favourite, but flowers of silk or parchment are also available and have the advantage of lasting a long time and of being hypoallergenic. They are, of course, more costly than the real thing.

> Symbolizing spring, and new life, flowers are a plea for fertility and healthy children. Often strong-smelling herbs were entwined with flowers, or even used by themselves, since it was thought that the strong smells would help to ward off bad luck, evil spirits and ill health.

Since there are so many ways of using flowers, and the time of year makes such a difference to cost, it is impossible to say what the total average expenditure is likely to be but, using seasonal flowers, a bridal bouquet is likely to cost around £30 to £60, a bridesmaid's spray about £15 to £30, buttonholes around £3.50 each and, as a rough guide, a 1.5 m (5 ft) pedestal display anything from £50 upwards.

There are specialist companies which will arrange for the bridal bouquet to be dried, pressed and mounted, as a permanent reminder and keepsake of the day. Prices vary, according to the size of the bouquet, the type of flowers used and the size of frame, but a good rule of thumb would be to allow between £50 to £100.

Cake

Using a local bakery, or the chef at the reception venue (if there is one) is the most convenient way to arrange for a wedding cake to be made. The baker will help to estimate what weight of cake will be needed to serve all guests a piece and leave enough to send to absent friends.

Generally the cake is chosen from a catalogue of photographs, and most bakers will mix and match decorations to individual requirements.

The modern wedding cake was introduced into England from France in the seventeenth century, probably by Royalists returning from exile when King Charles II was restored to his throne. One superstition holds that if the bride-to-be whispers to a beehive that she is to marry, the bees make especially sweet and powerful honey for the honeymoon drink, mead. In return she makes an offering to the hive of something sweet, such as the wedding cake with its sugar coating, from the wedding breakfast table.

Wedding cakes are generally rich fruit cakes but these are not to everyone's taste. One tier, made out of sponge cake, iced and decorated to match the fruit layers gives guests a choice.

Rich fruit cakes will last a long time, if stored properly, and will often taste better if allowed to mature. However, if the baker makes cakes well in advance and then stores them inadequately, they will be dry and lacking in flavour so ask to try a piece of one of his or her cakes before placing your order. A reputable baker should be happy to provide samples.

The baker, or the reception venue manager, should be able to supply a cake stand and slice for the wedding day. There may be an extra charge, but it is unlikely to be very much. The cost of the cake itself will depend on its size and the complexity of its decorations: a small two-tier cake should be around £150.

Stationery

Every good stationer and printer will have catalogues of wedding stationery. The range is huge, from the simplest card to the most comprehensive collection, from chocolate-box-pretty to supremely elegant.

Designs are pre-printed and there are generally several typefaces to choose from as well. Details of the wedding are sent to the printer with an order, which will take four to eight weeks to deliver, depending on the time of the year. Matched collections include:

- invitations to the church/civil venue only
- invitations to the ceremony and reception
- invitations to the reception only
- reply cards
- orders of service
- table name cards
- cake boxes
- table napkins
- book matches
- thank you cards.

There is generally a minimum order and prices start from around £40–£50 for a small run of simple cards.

Personalized stationery is becoming more common and certainly adds something to the image and ambiance of the occasion. If your *Yellow Pages*, under 'Wedding Services', does not have a listing for a stationery designer, ask a local printer and/or check the classified advertisements in your local paper. Bridal magazines are also a good source of information.

Commissioning a designer to create your wedding stationery is one way of putting a personal mark on a wedding. Designer stationery may take a little longer to deliver than pre-printed items, so taking into account that invitations should be sent out no later than six weeks before the wedding, and preferably eight to nine weeks before, a consultation with the designer should really take place around four or five months before the wedding.

Individual and unique cards allow you to use your own imagination. You might like to use your horoscopes, whether Western or Chinese style, or use a photograph (which can be scanned onto a card) or cartoon character (but take care not to infringe copyright).

Prices will be higher than for mass-produced stationery, but by how much will depend on the amount of work involved, the quality of the paper used and the number of items ordered. It is important to fix a deadline for completion and the price right at the beginning in order to avoid unpleasant surprises.

How many to order

You should allow sufficient numbers of invitations to the ceremony and reception, plus reply cards if they are being provided as a convenience to guests, so that one of each can be sent to:

- every family being invited (that is couples and their children under the age of 18 years)
- every married or engaged couple
- every individual (every person aged over 18 years of age, whether living alone, at their family home with parents or with a partner).

In addition keep spares for those last minute additions or those lost in the mail.

The term 'and friend' may be added to an invitation to individuals and they should include the name of the friend they intend to bring with them in the reply accepting the invitation.

If guests are to be invited only to the reception and not the ceremony, or to the ceremony but not to the reception, separate invitations and reply cards will be needed.

When ordering pre-printed stationery, discounts to prices are sometimes available for volume so it can be advantageous to make all the decisions, such as the form of the church service and the music that will be played for the order of service, and so on, and order a complete set of stationery all at once.

If the reception is to be held at a hotel, the function co-ordinator will probably offer place cards and napkins as part of the package. If the bride wishes to keep an overall theme by following through her own choice of stationery, the hotel may be willing to undertake the calligraphy work of making up the place cards, using the bride's own stationery, but are unlikely to offer a price reduction if both stationery and calligraphy are done elsewhere.

Fees

Register office fees are fixed by the Registrar General's office and apply throughout England, Wales and Northern Ireland. They are currently:

- £23 to be paid on giving Notice of Intent to Marry (or £23 each if parties live in different districts)

- £33 on the wedding day, plus
- £3.50 for a copy of the Register, i.e. the Marriage Certificate.

Church fees are not fixed and vary considerably around the country. Larger churches tend to charge more because they cost more to run and maintain. The following are guides:

Service	£50–£150
Organist	£20–£60
Flowers	£40–£100
Choir	£40–£100
Soloist	£20–£75
Facilities fee (for video)	£20–£80
Heating (in winter)	£20–£50
Bell ringers	£20–£100

The cost of the Marriage Certificate will almost always be included in the basic service fee but the registrar's fees may not. If the ceremony is held in any other church than an Anglican church, the registrar may charge for travel/extra time and so on, so always check with the district registrar's office or the minister/priest concerned.

Not every church charges separately for all these different services. Some will include the services of an organist, the heating and some flower arrangements (two pedestals, for example) in the basic fee and some will not charge a facilities fee to video recorders. Always ask, however, because it is amazing how these little extras mount up!

Insurance

This is an absolute must and any broker will be able to find a company to provide a suitable policy and advise you when to take it out. Only one or two insurance companies handle wedding insurance, so shopping around probably will not help reduce costs, but premiums are fairly modest so this should not be a problem. Expect premiums to be around £50 for basic cover, with extras available to suit different circumstances.

A recommended minimum level of cover should include:

- loss, theft, damage to/of any item of clothing (bridal gown, bridesmaids' dresses, accessories and menswear, whether bought or hired)
- loss, damage or failure of photographs, howsoever caused
- illness or death of bride or groom or parent of either

- failure of any contracted supplier to provide the goods or services agreed upon at the time of agreed delivery
- loss, theft or damage to/of wedding presents
- loss, theft or damage to/of wedding rings.

No insurance company will insure against anyone changing their mind, whether it is an attendant, one or both of the bridal couple, or a parent of either of them.

Cover is usually restricted to the cost of replacement, but it is worth asking if additional cover, such as compensation for stress, or for extra expenses incurred as a result of any loss or damage, might also be included in a policy.

An insurance policy proved invaluable when the bride's father had a heart attack the day before the wedding. The wedding was postponed since the family's concern throughout that night and the next few days was concentrated on him. Fortunately he recovered well and the wedding went ahead at a later date. The insurance policy covered the costs of cancelling the catered reception and flowers, reprinting the stationery, and lost deposits on transport, photography, video recording, menswear hire and entertainment. Dresses, accessories and the cake were all used at the rescheduled wedding, three months later.

Wedding arrangers

If you have only limited time to devote to arranging your wedding, prefer to have your wedding arranged by professionals, are unsure whether you can do the job well enough, or feel that other people's well-meaning advice (or dare we say, interference) is more than you can cope with, then employing an arranger might be the answer.

Most companies which advertise this service are actually information bureaux, acting as agents and sending out information on all kinds of wedding services under their own corporate banner. It is then up to the client to make contact directly with suppliers and conclude arrangements. Generally this is offered as a free service and, in a way, it is since the enquirer/client is not charged directly for the information provided. However, companies promoted by agents in this way pay a commission, or introduction fee, a cost which they must recover somehow. It almost invariably turns up in the client's bill, hidden in the overall charges.

Companies that offer a genuine arrangement service, that is those that choreograph the whole wedding from beginning to end, are few and far between in the United Kingdom at present, although they are common in other countries, particularly the United States. These companies may have a financial arrangement with the suppliers of wedding services they use in arranging a client's wedding, or they may charge the client a fee, based on the size and shape of the wedding.

In this latter system, the arrangers are free to use any supplier they, or the client, wishes since their own financial advantage is not a factor. As well as giving more choice, this may also mean lower costs since the businesses used have a vested interest (the possibility of repeat business from the arranger) to encourage them to deliver quality and value.

Gifts

Gift list

Few brides and grooms are entirely comfortable with the principle of a wedding gift list but it is a boon to guests, allowing them to choose something they know the couple wants within a price range they can afford.

If the newly-weds are setting up a completely new home, the list will almost certainly be a long one, containing expensive items as well as the relatively inexpensive. If their home is already established they may need very little or they may list items to replace those which are old and/or worn. Whatever the situation, the wedding gift list should be as comprehensive as possible so that guests have plenty of choice. Even expensive items should be included since it gives the opportunity for people to club together for a gift really worth giving, if they wish.

There are several ways of handling a gift list to ensure it receives a wide circulation. The bride may choose a shop with branches nationwide and visit the manager of her local store to find out whether they are able to handle her list. She then sends a copy of the list to every guest. The guest visits or telephones their own local branch of the store and chooses a gift. The company checks that that particular item has not been chosen already by someone else, then wraps it and delivers it to the bride's home, with a suitable card. If the gift has been chosen by someone else, a message goes back to the guest asking them to choose again.

Some stores will perform this service without charge, because of the benefits of business it brings them, but some will charge a fee.

Another way is to split the list into three or four equal parts and send each part, with the names of one-third or one-quarter of the guests, to one guest whose name should appear at the top of the guest list. This person chooses the gift they will send, crosses off their own name from the list along with the item they have chosen to give, and sends the list on to the person named next.

Probably the simplest alternative is for the bride or her mother to manage the list themselves. A copy of the list goes out to every invited guest who then calls the bride or her mother to discuss their choice and check that someone else has not already made the same choice.

Good manners suggest that, whichever method of managing the list is chosen, it should not be released until after invitations have been sent out. Too soon and the invitation takes on a rather mercenary complexion and too late may create difficulties in managing it successfully. A week or two later would be ideal. Everyone needs to know how the list is being managed and guidance should be included with each copy sent out.

Parents' gifts

Not quite a tradition yet, it is common for the couple to give presents to their parents. The gifts should commemorate the day, reflecting the couple's love and thanks for the years of care their parents have given them. Suggestions include engraved crystal, ornamental photograph frames (perhaps silver) or the bridal bouquet, dried and mounted in a picture frame, or a piece of porcelain.

Attendants' gifts

The bride and groom normally give a small gift to each of their attendants in order to thank them for what they have done. As far as possible, the gift should have some connection with the wedding and be personal to the recipient.

For a church wedding, the gifts may be, for example, a prayer book with an inscription from the bride and groom, a piece of jewellery, such as a pendant cross or crucifix or an illuminated scroll commemorating the day. The bridal couple usually present the gifts before the wedding so they may be used (the prayer book) or worn (jewellery) on the day.

Honeymoon

A honeymoon is an opportunity to wind down from the nervous tension and excitement of preparation and the wedding day and, with so many travel companies offering packaged holidays at moderate prices, it needn't cost the earth.

Traditionally the honeymoon is taken immediately after the wedding and arranging it is the groom's responsibility. If the honeymoon is to be spent in the United Kingdom the couple may wish to travel on the day of the wedding, leaving the reception to do so, driving off into the sunset with confetti blowing everywhere and tin cans tied to the rear bumper of the car.

Most honeymoons nowadays are of two or three weeks' duration, not the original 'moon', or lunar month, of earlier tradition. Even so, a change of pace and place after the adrenaline rush of the countdown to a wedding day, is generally most welcome. A honeymoon can be romantic almost anywhere, whether it is spent ten miles from home or half-way around the world.

Going abroad is a little less convenient, since the majority of holiday flights leave at inconvenient times of the day and, often, midweek. In this case, the favoured option is to spend the wedding night in the hotel which hosted the reception, or one very close by, and travel the next day. Some newly-weds postpone the honeymoon until a more convenient time, or may opt not to take one at all. It's not unusual for children to go on honeymoon with their newly-wed parents and some couples even take parents or other relatives with them.

Arranging a honeymoon is no different from arranging any other sort of trip in that reservations must be made, visas applied for (where appropriate), passports obtained (if needed and/or not already held) and health checks/precautions carried out. If the wedding is to be held during a busy holiday season, such as the period between mid-July and the end of August, or over Christmas or Easter, then reservations are best made early, say around seven to eight months before the wedding, especially if the destination is popular.

The honeymoon is so called because mead, a strongly alcoholic drink made of fermented honey, was served to newly-weds during the first month (or moon) of their married life. It was said to promote fertility and early conception. A modern cynic may say this had as much to do with the loosening of inhibitions brought about by copious amounts of alcohol than by any magical properties of the brew!

If the bride already holds her own passport it will not be necessary to change it to show her married name. She may continue to use it until it expires, but should keep her marriage certificate with it while travelling in order to avoid any possible confusion.

If you are planning to go abroad, check early with your GP if any vaccinations are required. The last thing you need is to be suffering the after effects of a vaccination on the wedding day, if you cut it too fine. Your GP might also help you rearrange your menstrual cycle. Consult him or her in plenty of time, if you think it might impact badly on the honeymoon!

04

budgeting and booking

Setting the budget

By now you will have a good idea of what sort of wedding you want and should have a working budget to begin with. You will alter and refine your plans continually over the next few months, so be prepared to be flexible while still keeping your objectives clear in your mind.

Planning a wedding isn't difficult, but you'll need some organizational skill and a lot of patience. In this chapter we look at the main aspects of the wedding, and identify the people you should see, and talk to, and how to keep it all under control.

Without a doubt, a wedding is quite possibly the single most expensive event that a family or individual is likely to arrange. The preparation of any budget calls for information and a wedding budget is no different, it is a matter of knowing what is needed, (keeping a little flexibility in reserve just in case your first choice is already booked, is too expensive or is simply not available) and researching the options carefully. Remember, the client writes the cheques: if a supplier is not satisfactory in some way, look for another.

Ask friends for recommendations, use the *Yellow Pages* and local newspapers, call in at local shops. Some providers will send photographs (of cars, for example), some will ask if they can meet you to discuss your needs and some will suggest a visit to their shops or offices. Explain the requirement fully and ask for estimates – check that like is being comparing with like and bear in mind that price may not always be a good guide to quality.

With a mental picture of the wedding in mind, or better still, a written plan, it is quite easy to add figures against the key elements. The resulting budget will provide a very rough figure of the sort of costs to be expected. The emphasis here is on 'rough' because suppliers will be unable to guarantee estimates until firm commitments are made, with dates, times, numbers and so on, and a deposit is paid. As a rough guide, a traditional church wedding for around 100 guests will cost approximately £8,000 to £15,000, excluding honeymoon. It can be achieved for less (should your budget be tight); you could also spend more (if money is no object) and we will show you how to do both in later chapters. Register office weddings tend to be less formal and more relaxed, and so tend to cost less. An average cost for 60 guests would be around £3,500 to £4,500.

Example 1

A Church of England wedding, with 100 guests, is planned for late morning, with a reception to be held at a local golf club. There will be four bridesmaids (two adults and two children) and four ushers. The bridesmaids will meet at the bride's home where a beauty therapist and a hairdresser will do the bride's make-up and hair.

The bride and her father will travel to the church in an Edwardian landau, pulled by two horses and attended by two footmen in appropriate period outfits. It will wait at the church to take the newly-weds to the reception after the ceremony. A limousine will be hired to take the bridesmaids and the bride's mother to the church, and then make two trips to the reception, with the bride's parents and then with the bridesmaids. The bridal car is to return later, first to take the couple to a hotel for their wedding night, and then to take the bride's parents and the chief bridesmaid home, with the wedding presents and remainder of the cake.

The bride will carry a large bouquet of roses and evergreens, with a fresh-flower headdress to match. Each bridesmaid has a small, hand-held posy. The florist will provide two pedestal arrangements for the church and 24 posies for pew ends. The groom, best man, the bride's father and ushers will all wear buttonhole flowers.

Guests will be welcomed to the reception with a glass of buck's fizz and then sit down to a silver service three-course meal, plus coffee and mints. Wine will be served with the meal and pieces of a three-tier wedding cake will be served during the speeches, with a glass of champagne for the toasts. The club bar, where guests buy their own drinks, opens when the tables have been cleared. In the late afternoon 30 of the guests leave, but 40 more arrive to join an evening celebration, with a live band and a disco, that continues until around 11 p.m.

Budget

Bridal gown and accessories	£1,400.00
Bridesmaids' outfits (purchased)	£450.00
Beauty therapist/hairdresser (bride only)	£100.00
Menswear (groom, best man, bride's father and ushers), hired	£600.00
Flowers	£400.00
Photographer	£750.00

Transport, horse-drawn carriage		£1,000.00
Cars		£450.00
Stationery and postage		£550.00
Rings		£200.00
Cake		£250.00
Reception		£6,500.00
Entertainment		£500.00
Going-away outfits		£400.00
Fees (church)		£300.00
Insurance		£100.00
	Total	£13,950.00
Honeymoon		£2,500.00

Example 2

A register office wedding at mid-morning, with 60 guests, is to be followed by a short reception at a local hotel. A hired limousine takes the bride and her sister to the register office and, after the ceremony, takes the newly-weds to the reception. The groom will be accompanied by a friend, who will stand as one of the witnesses and the bride will enter the register office with her sister, who will stand as the other. The bride and her sister both carry posies of seasonal flowers. The bridal couple have provided a music tape to be played during the ceremony.

The reception will be held at a local hotel where guests will be welcomed with a glass of sherry. Taped music will play in the background and a finger buffet, with wine, is provided. The bar is open for those who wish to purchase other types of drinks. Speeches are made and the cake is cut and a glass of champagne is provided for everyone for the toasts.

The newly-weds leave at 3 p.m. for their honeymoon at an English country cottage in the New Forest.

Budget

Bridal gown and accessories	£500.00
Sister's outfit	£150.00
Menswear (2), purchased	£400.00
Reception	£2,000.00
Transport	£300.00
Rings	£180.00
Cake	£140.00
Photographer	£500.00

Stationery and postage		£200.00
Fees		£85.00
Flowers		£50.00
Insurance		£40.00
	Total	£4,545.00
Honeymoon		£650.00

These are just two examples and the possible variations are enormous. A church wedding need not cost anywhere near this much or, if you wish it to, can cost much, much more. A ceremony in an Anglican Church, shared by a few friends and family, using the flowers already in the church as decoration, with friends taking photographs and dressing up your own specially cleaned and polished car, followed by lunch at a local hotel afterwards, can be had for £1,000. On the other hand, famous people have been known to fly in guests from all over the world, host parties that go on for days and spend money with six zeros on the end.

Register offices give more potential for economy but that is not the only reason for choosing this venue, of course. Still, a small group at a register office with a posy or two of flowers, some music on tape, a pretty outfit and a party at home afterwards need cost no more than £400–£500 and you will be just as married!

When to pay

You will almost always be asked for a deposit when you agree to buy goods or services. The trader will ask you to sign an agreement, or contract, which will also serve as a receipt for your deposit. The price you agree now should be the price you actually pay. Most weddings are planned around nine to twelve months in advance and any intended price rises should be already included in the price you are quoted. Check that this is the case before you pay a deposit. Above all, make sure you read the contract carefully; once you have signed it and the deposit is paid there will be a penalty should you change your mind. Most commonly this is the loss of your deposit.

The deposit may be anything between a token flat rate up to 20 to 30 per cent of the full price or estimated final cost. It is also quite common to be asked to pay the balance before the wedding day, a month before is the most usual. Deposits will generally be non-refundable although some traders will return a deposit if the cancellation allows sufficient time for another booking to be taken.

Some will ask for stage payments, for example, the caterer may ask for a booking deposit, another payment a month or so before the wedding and a final payment when final numbers are known and this, too, is fairly common. Check each trader's policy before booking.

Staged payments may be spread out over several months, making the cost of expensive parts of the wedding a little easier to meet, but there are risks attached. A reliable trader should deposit your advance payments in a special client-account and keep a check on how much you have paid and how much/when expenditure has been incurred on your behalf. If this facility is not available, you would be wise to reconsider a trader's request for advance or staged payments.

Loans

It is possible to borrow money from banks and finance houses to pay for a wedding, in the same way that money for a new car or furniture can be borrowed. Most commonly this is done through a personal loan secured by an approved asset, such as property or a life assurance policy. Interest rates vary according to the prevailing financial climate but, once arranged, are fixed for the term of repayments which may be anything but are usually one to five years.

It is wise to get approval in principle for a loan well in advance, then arrange to draw on the facility only when expenditure is at its highest, otherwise you could find yourself paying interest on borrowed money that sits in a bank account for weeks, or months, before it is really needed.

Insurance

One expense that may seem to be low priority but is, in fact, very important, is the insurance cover. It won't cover against either the bride or groom changing their mind but it should cover accidents, losses and thefts to clothes, people and facilities, or failure of suppliers to deliver contracted services, which may prevent the wedding going ahead or being completed satisfactorily.

Liability will be limited to specific maximum values and cover will come into force only at a predetermined date of so many weeks before the wedding date.

05

different types
of ceremonies

The official requirements for getting married in the United Kingdom are covered in Chapter 1. In this chapter we will look (in alphabetical order) at the various religious ceremonies of different faiths. Elements from different faiths, such as customs and tradition, can be adopted when designing your own ceremony. If you decide upon a traditional ceremony, there are ways in which this can be adapted to suit your situation and personalities. (Ways to develop your own personal ceremony are discussed in Chapter 6.)

Anglican

Ushers

Ushers should be the first to arrive at the church, around 40 minutes before the ceremony is to take place. The best man should have made sure, in advance, that the ushers know how to seat the guests, have enough orders of service (where appropriate), and prayer and hymn books for everyone.

Seats in the front pew on the right-hand side should be reserved for the groom and his best man, with the groom's family seated alongside and immediately behind, in the second pew. The front pew on the left is reserved for the bride's parents and the bride's attendants. Guests will begin to arrive 15–20 minutes before the service and ushers show them to their seats; bride's family to the left and groom's to the right.

Close family of the bride and groom are seated at the front, directly behind parents and attendants, graduating to other relatives and then friends in pews further back. The best man should have checked out the local parking situation in advance and, if there is a problem, the ushers should be briefed beforehand.

Bridesmaids and bride's mother

The next to arrive are the bridesmaids and the bride's mother. The bride's mother will probably wait with the bridesmaids at the church entrance until the bride's car arrives, especially if any of the bridesmaids are very young, but she should be seated in her place, in front row on the left-hand side, before the bride actually enters the church.

Overheard at a recent wedding, bridesmaid (bride's sister, aged six) to bride's mum: 'How will he know it's really her mummy? He's never seen her in a dress before!'

Arrival of the bride

At the bride's home, the chauffeur should escort the bride and her father to the car which should be parked so that the bride can enter and sit directly behind the front passenger seat without needing to shuffle across the rear seat or walk out into the road. This puts her on her father's left-hand side as he sits behind the chauffeur.

On arrival at the church the chauffeur should pull up so that the bride can alight directly, again so that she does not need to shuffle across the seat. The chauffeur should first open the door for the bride's father to alight, then they both walk round the rear of the car and the chauffeur opens the door for the bride. Her father helps her alight and then offers her his left arm as they walk up the church path to the entrance. If it is raining the chauffeur should escort his passengers to the church entrance with an umbrella.

Traditionally, a lady is always placed on the left-hand side of a gentleman so that, as they walk, his right hand is free to draw and use his sword in the event of trouble. How left-handed gentlemen managed is not explained!

At the church door the bridesmaids help the bride to make sure her gown, veil and headdress are neatly arranged and secure before they take their places behind her, in pairs with the youngest first, and begin their progress up the aisle. If the bridesmaids lead the way, with the bride and her father following, the oldest bridesmaids go first, with the youngest closest to the bride.

As the bride and her father enter the church they should pause to give one of the ushers time to signal to the minister/priest that the bride is ready. At the usher's signal, the organist begins to play the music chosen for the progress and the groom and best man leave their seats to stand in front of the chancel steps, facing the minister/priest, waiting for the bride and her father to join them.

At the chancel steps

On arrival at the chancel steps the bride releases her father's arm and he moves to take up his position on her left, a small pace behind her, with the groom on her right-hand side. The best man stands on the groom's right, a small pace behind him. The bride hands her flowers, and anything else she is carrying, including gloves, to her chief bridesmaid or matron-of-honour so that her hands are free. If there are no attendants, she hands these items to her father who gives them to her mother, seated in the front pew on his left. The bridesmaids and other attendants seat themselves with the bride's mother in the front pew, left-hand side.

The minister/priest begins the ceremony with a short address, reminding the congregation of the solemnity of the occasion and that it is a happy event for the families and for the couple who are bringing them together through matrimony. Guests follow the service with their orders of service or prayer books, as appropriate.

After the minister has asked the bride and groom separately whether they will each take the other as spouse, the minister asks 'Who giveth this woman to be married to this man?' The bride's father steps forward saying 'I do', takes her right hand in his and places it, palm down, in the minister's hand. The minister then places her hand in the groom's right hand and the symbolic gesture of 'giving away' the bride is complete.

Giving away the bride is a tradition that goes back to long before the emancipation of women, to a time when a single girl belonged to her father in much the same way as did a dog or a horse. Any property or wealth she owned was her father's to control in any way he saw fit since it was widely believed that a woman's brain was incapable of dealing with matters of business and finance. In Victorian times a single woman could take control of her own property once she reached the age of 30 (although in reality many fathers never let go of the reins), at which age she also no longer needed parental consent to marry. Convention decreed, however, that permission should still be sought and the father's opinion was given great weight. On her marriage, at whatever age, her husband took over control of her property, taking over where her father, or she herself, had left off. Even if she was 30 or older, and had already experienced the responsibility of controlling her own assets, she was still bound, by law, to give control to her husband on her marriage. The present symbolic act of 'giving away the bride' had, at this time, a very real and literal meaning since marriage involved her father giving both her and her property, quite literally, into the total control of her new husband.

With prior arrangement with the minister this part of the ceremony may be omitted, and it often is nowadays, largely because, even as a tradition, it can be an emotive issue. Sometimes it is omitted because the bride has no-one to stand with her in the father's role and she prefers not to have a substitute, or if the couple are older and the words are not appropriate for their situation.

Vows and rings

The bride and groom now exchange their vows and rings. The best man places the rings on the minister's prayer book under the minister's guidance. After the exchange of vows and rings, the couple are declared husband and wife and are invited to kiss to seal the ceremony. Many congregations applaud at this point and most ministers/priests are delighted to join in.

The ring symbolizes the cycle of life, death and rebirth promised by Christ and of the never-ending nature of the marriage vows. Gold represents the indestructible nature of marriage since gold is the only natural metal that never rusts, changes or loses its sheen. The ring is placed on the third finger of the left hand because this was thought to be linked, through some form of life force, with the heart, the seat of emotion. Modern medicine, and an improved knowledge of anatomy, has disproved this belief, but the tradition continues anyway, at least in Western culture. Rings worn on the right or left hand, a jewel worn in a pierced nose, head gear which hides a woman's hair and many other ways signal a woman's marital status in different cultures.

At this point the bride's father takes his seat in the front pew with the bride's mother, and the best man takes his seat in the front pew on the right-hand side of the aisle. The couple now kneel at the chancel steps to receive the blessing and, after prayers and, perhaps, a hymn, the minister/priest leads them to the altar. If there is to be a communion, it may be made at this point, or at the end of the marriage service which is concluded with prayers and a hymn as the minister/priest stands before the altar.

The newly married couple, their parents, (bride's mother first, escorted by the groom's father, then the groom's mother escorted by the bride's father) the chief bridesmaid or matron-of-honour and the best man now go into the vestry, with the minister, to sign the register. If the vestry is large enough to admit all the bride's attendants, they should also go with the group, bringing up the rear. In the vestry, the Marriage Certificate (a copy of the register entry) is completed and given to the couple. In the body of the church, the choir and/or organist perform for the congregation.

The bride retrieves her flowers from the chief bridesmaid or matron-of-honour and the party leaves the vestry to re-enter the body of the church.

Leaving the church

The procession forms behind the couple as they walk down the aisle. The flower girl (if there is one) walks ahead of the bride and groom scattering flower petals as she goes. After the bride and groom, the pageboy and ring bearer follow together, both now carrying the train (if applicable), followed by the best man and chief bridesmaid or matron-of-honour, then ushers paired with bridesmaids. The bride's mother walks with the groom's father, and the groom's mother walks with the bride's father as they follow the attendants, with family and friends following on in turn, from the front pews first, as the procession passes.

> Confetti is a modern substitute for rice, or other grain seeds, which were scattered over the bride and groom, and beneath their feet, to invoke a life of plenty and freedom from hunger, being a symbol of growth and successful harvest.

Video and photography

The general view is that flashes and clicks during the ceremony can be very distracting, for the minister as well as for everyone else, and so many of the clergy refuse permission to photograph or record the ceremony itself. Ushers should tell guests carrying cameras, as they arrive, whether they can use them in the church.

Depending on what the minister/priest has agreed both photographer and video maker should arrive at the church with plenty of time to set up for shots of the interior before the ceremony. Both should take steps to ensure that, whatever shots they take, their presence does not intrude into the service in any way.

Outside, after the ceremony the photographer arranges guests for group pictures, with the help of the ushers, and takes individual and paired shots of the bride and groom. Although guests should never leave before the bridal couple, a wet or cold day will see some begin to drift away in twos and small groups, if the photographer takes too long with his or her task. It is the best man's duty to make sure this doesn't happen.

> A winter wedding can leave a bride almost blue with cold and even in summer, a thin silky dress can be decidedly chilly on a blustery day. If the bride would prefer to be somewhere warmer, she should say so. Alternatively, thermal underwear is light and very pretty nowadays, just the job for cooler days.

Since the photographic session can take some while to complete, the video maker will generally be ready to leave first, giving him or her the opportunity to set up equipment at the reception to record the bridal couple arriving.

Blessing services

If you are divorced, are marrying for the second time and wish to have an Anglican service to celebrate the wedding in a church where the vicar will not solemnize the marriage, a service of blessing is a good alternative option. The content and style of the service is very much at the discretion of the minister and the couple, and there may be a good deal of scope for writing your own ceremony.

As a general rule, the couple walk down the aisle together at the beginning of the service, or if she has not been married before, the bride may be escorted to join the groom who is waiting at the altar, whilst the congregation are singing the first hymn. The couple will then make their promises in front of the congregation as they have already done at a previous civil ceremony.

Buddhist

Buddhism is a religion and philosophy affecting much of the cultural, spiritual and social life of the Eastern world. The focus of Buddhism is an individual's quest for inner salvation through a spiritual journey towards perfection. Everything, other than the inner entity, is considered to be temporary.

Weddings under the Buddhist faith are very rare, since strictly speaking there is no prescribed wedding ceremony. However, it is possible to construct an individual civil ceremony reflecting the couple's cultural traditions, and for a blessing to be undertaken by a Buddhist priest.

Catholic

All marriages outside the Church of England require a licence. The couple must give notice of their intention to marry to the local superintendent registrar. Usually the priest is authorized to register the marriage; if not, a registrar will need to be present.

The Catholic Church still considers marriage between a person of the Catholic faith and a person of another faith as a 'mixed' marriage. However, the Catholic Church is more liberal now than it used to be and does not impose such strict conditions as it used to if such a couple wants to marry in a Catholic ceremony. Even so, you will need to visit the Priest and discuss your plans in plenty of time because there are still many aspects to consider which might not have occurred to you.

With regard to the ceremony, open discussion with both ministers should assist. For example, if the bride is Church of England and the groom is Catholic and they decide to marry in the Bride's church, an arrangement may be made for the groom's priest to attend and give the bride his blessing.

The ceremony

As mentioned above, if both parties are Roman Catholic, the ceremony usually forms part of a full nuptial mass. The elements of the service cover the significance of marriage, declarations that there are no lawful reasons why the couple may not marry, and promises of faithfulness to each other and the couple's acceptance to bring up children within the Roman Catholic faith.

Once the bride has walked up the aisle, the service begins with a hymn and a Bible reading, followed by a sermon. The priest then asks whether there is any impediment to the marriage and calls on the couple to give their consent 'according to the rite of our holy mother the Church' to which each responds 'I will'. The couple join right hands and call upon the congregation to witness the marriage and then they make their vows to cherish one another. Vows are exchanged, the priest confirms them in marriage and the best man hands over the ring(s) which are blessed and given or exchanged, with the couple acknowledging them as a token of their love and fidelity. In addition to the ring, the groom gives gold and silver to the bride as tokens of his worldly goods. Once the rings are blessed, the groom places the ring first on the bride's thumb, and then on three fingers in turn. Bidding prayers, nuptial blessing and possibly Holy Communion and Thanksgiving follow. After the final blessing is the dismissal, whereupon the bride, groom and bridal party move into the sacristy to make the civil declaration, and to sign and witness the register. If there is to be a following nuptial mass, the bridesmaids take their places in a reserved pew at the front.

For the nuptial mass, the couple return to the sanctuary, and kneel; the bride is assisted by the groom. If Holy Communion is to be received, those taking it move forward at the appropriate time, returning to their pews afterwards. When the Mass ends, the couple proceed down the aisle from the sanctuary, followed by the chief bridesmaid and best man, and then the other bridesmaids, pageboys and parents before the rest of the guests.

Christian Scientist

Christian Scientist churches may be licensed for marriage ceremonies, if the minister has registered with the local authority. The minister is not generally, however, a registrar. If the building is registered, and the minister is not a registrar, then a registrar from the local office will need to perform the legal requirements of the service. If the church is not registered, the legal ceremony will have to be held at the register office, or some other licensed place. A religious service can still be held at the church, of course, it just won't fulfil the legal requirement on its own.

Church of Scotland

The marriage ceremony is very similar to that of the Church of England. The main difference is that, provided the ceremony is conducted by an authorized minister of the Church of Scotland, and under Scottish Law, you can be married anywhere, in or outside a building, whether a religious venue or not.

Hindu

The bride wears a red silk sari, and the groom is dressed in white. All attending the wedding wear their smartest, and most colourful, clothing to celebrate the wedding.

The ceremony itself is very informal, with guests chatting amongst themselves and generally enjoying themselves whilst it is going on. If the building in which the ceremony is to take place is registered to hold weddings, couples should give notice of their intention to marry so that a registrar may attend to register the marriage. If the building does not hold a licence, a civil wedding will be required beforehand.

At the wedding venue, the bride's family will arrange a sacred place, covered with a canopy of richly decorated material and flowers in the middle of the room.

The bride will arrive first, and hides until the groom and remaining guests have assembled. As the groom enters, lights are waved over his head and grains of rice thrown to symbolize wealth and fertility. The groom takes his place under the canopy, at which time his bride joins him. The wedding ceremony gets underway, and may last all day with gifts being given and food eaten throughout the celebration.

Humanist

Many people today do not hold the traditional religious beliefs. However, they often want to enter a committed marriage, and wish to celebrate this with a ceremony to mark the rite of passage.

If you feel uneasy about entering your marriage with a religious ceremony that does not mean anything to you, and yet you do not wish merely to go through a register office wedding with no personal content or emotional satisfaction, a Humanist wedding could be the answer.

Humanists now have a national network of trained officiants. They have produced a booklet entitled *Sharing the Future* which outlines their aims, and gives information on sample ceremonies and readings. You could choose to adopt a ceremony encompassing your own values and beliefs, or you may adopt a very traditional ceremony, but omit the religious elements.

By contacting the Humanist Association (see Taking it further), you can locate your nearest officiant; alternatively, you may choose a family friend or relative to conduct the ceremony. The basic focus of the service is on commitment, love and respect for each other. If either or both of the couple have children, the couple's commitment and love for the children is reflected in the service. A number of readings and poetry may be included.

A ceremony could take the following form:

- a welcome to guests, and stating of the reasons behind the couple's choosing a Humanist ceremony
- readings by the couple, friends and family about marriage, love and commitment
- vows made by the couple to each other and any children, either written by themselves or adapted from the traditional vows
- exchange of rings or other tokens, such as candles, the sharing of wine, etc.
- families possibly joining in the ceremony by offering their support of the couple
- readings or poems read by the couple or their family and friends about the future and their lives together.

Inter-faith marriages

Religion and culture are very often inter-connected, and marrying someone of a different faith can be problematic. With thorough discussion and communication you can generally overcome many of the problems between yourselves; however, with your family it may be a little different.

Different faiths also have different views on inter-faith marriages; the Catholic Church will allow marriage to other Christians by dispensation; Orthodox Jews will not allow it under any circumstances; Muslims will expect non-Muslims to convert; other faiths, such as Unitarians, are much more tolerant.

Many couples from different faiths manage to keep the peace with their families by having two ceremonies. This is particularly appropriate when one of the beliefs would require a separate civil ceremony in order to be legally recognized. Alternatively, you may choose to design your own ceremony, drawing on elements from both faiths.

Jewish

According to civil law in the United Kingdom, a Jewish marriage may be solemnized in any building, at any time of the day, provided the couple have obtained the necessary legal documentation from the registrar. Jewish weddings are solemnized either in an Orthodox synagogue under the authority of the Chief Rabbi, or in a Progressive synagogue where the civil authority appoints a marriage secretary who is responsible for the legal side of the ceremony.

For a couple to marry under the Jewish faith, both the bride and groom must be Jews. If one of the couple is not Jewish, they must undertake a formal conversion prior to the wedding.

Jewish weddings cannot be solemnized at any time between sunset on Friday to sunset on Saturday (the Jewish Sabbath) – most weddings take place on Sundays. At the wedding, the bridegroom and all men present must wear hats, and the bride will wear a veil. In all Orthodox and most Progressive synagogues, women should have their heads covered.

Prior to the wedding, the couple are likely to be requested to visit the rabbi for pre-marital counselling.

The ceremony

The groom will arrive at the synagogue with his father and best man who will give him away. When the bride arrives, the groom is escorted under a *chuppah* (a silk or velvet canopy, supported by poles, possibly decorated with flowers).

The bride is led into the synagogue on the arm of her father, followed by the bridesmaids and mothers of the couple. The bride stands to the right of the groom under the *chuppah* and the wedding ceremony commences with a blessing given by the minister.

After the ceremony, the couple will be left alone in the synagogue room – for a quick embrace, before joining the festivities. At the reception, the rabbi will say grace in Hebrew before and after the meal, which will consist of Kosher food. At Orthodox wedding receptions, the men dance around in a big circle between courses, holding handkerchiefs so that they do not touch one another. The bride and groom are carried on chairs around the room. Jewish weddings are extremely rowdy, and joyful occasions, with much singing and dancing.

Muslim

A Muslim bride is dressed in a heavily decorated gown, with many jewels, which may be any colour, but is generally red. Female guests should have their legs and head covered, although their faces and hands may be visible.

In the United Kingdom, it will be necessary to ensure that all the civil requirements for marriage are undertaken. This will involve either a civil ceremony prior to the Muslim service, or, if the mosque is registered to hold wedding ceremonies, arranging for a registrar to attend to register the marriage.

Under Muslim beliefs, marriage is a contract, and not a sacrament, and thus any lay Muslim male may conduct the ceremony. Women are seated on one side of the mosque, with the men on the other. The service begins with a sermon, and is followed by readings from the Koran. The bride and groom give their consent to marry, and are pronounced man and wife. There are further prayers and a sermon before guests move onto the bride's parents' home.

The bride's parents host a reception, at which guests of the bride bring presents. A week later the groom's parents host another reception, at which the groom's relations and friends bring gifts. If this is not practical, the bride's family could host a party for a couple of hours, before moving straight onto the groom's family home to end the celebrations.

Non-conformist

This term includes Methodist, Baptist, Congregationalist, United Reformed and Assemblies of God faiths. Their services are similar to that offered by the Church of England, but they are often more flexible in their approach to the ceremony. They are more likely to be open to innovation.

Such churches are generally not licensed to perform marriage ceremonies, and thus a registrar may have to be present at the service to register the marriage with the minister conducting the ceremony.

Pagan

There are several forms of Pagan wedding from a New Age Handfasting to the formal Druid wedding rite. Pagans honour equality, and the unity of humankind with nature.

Handfasting is the old Anglo-Saxon word for an agreement between two people – shaking hands over an agreement is still done today, and the joining of hands is common in many marriage ceremonies. Many other symbols of marriage may be included in the ceremony, such as the sharing of bread and wine, jumping over a broomstick into a new life together, and the exchange of tokens or rings. Weddings are generally held out of doors within a circle so that the congregation may be close to nature, and may be presided over by a priest or priestess.

Druid ceremonies are attended by a druid or druidess. The guests form a horseshoe, within which the participants of the ceremony form a circle, again generally out of doors. Four 'gates' on the four points of the compass divide the circle.

The ceremony involves the celebrants calling on heaven and earth to witness the marriage, before the couple make their vows. The party walk to the four gates, embracing the elements that it represents – fire, water, earth and air. Vows and tokens (rings) are exchanged, and a candle lit. The couple walk around the circle to be greeted by those present as man and wife, before they make a central circle. Close family and friends make a second circle around them, and the remaining guests join hands to make a final third circle of existence, before a final blessing.

The full ceremony is described in the book *The Druid Way* by Philip Carr-Gomm, available from the Pagan Federation.

Quaker (Religious Society of Friends)

Quaker weddings can take place at any time of the day, and any venue, be it private house, hall or elsewhere. However, the usual place is in the Meeting House normally attended by either or both of the couple. Quaker marriages are a Christian commitment, not a civil alternative, and Quakers, like the Anglican Church, can register their own marriages. However, if the venue you choose is not licensed, a civil ceremony will also be required.

Marriage by couples where a previous marriage has ended in divorce are not forbidden, as long as the couple are sincere in their desire for a religious ceremony.

The couple are required to write to their local Meeting House, advising of their intention to marry. A meeting is then held between the couple, and a small group of men and women who are appointed to discuss the ceremony and its implications.

The service itself is very simple, with no procession, music, minister or pre-planned format. The couple sit at the front of the meeting house, facing the congregation. The bride is most likely to wear her best dress rather than a wedding gown, and the groom a grey suit with a buttonhole.

Weddings guests may stand and speak at any time, and when they feel the time is right, the couple will stand and state their vows, which have been agreed in advance with the elders. After they have made their promises, they will return to their seats and the meeting continues until the elders shake hands to signify that the ceremony is over. Rings may be exchanged at any time, but could take place during the reciting of the vows, or at the signing of the register.

Everyone attending the ceremony will follow onto the reception.

Single-sex partnerships

Both male and female homosexuals form long-term relationships which in all other respects are similar to a marriage. It is not unusual, therefore, for such couples to want their partnership to be recognized, although marriage between single-sex couples is not recognized in the United Kingdom.

If you wish to have your partnership formally recognized, you may choose to marry abroad where countries that have partnership laws make it possible to marry under civil law. These include Greenland, Iceland, Denmark, Norway, Sweden, Holland some American states (for example, California, where a 'Declaration of Domestic Partnership' is available).

The Metropolitan Community Church of Los Angeles is a church which celebrates the union of and gives a blessing for single-sex couples and transsexuals. Often their celebrants may be willing to travel to conduct ceremonies at a location of your choice. Originating in 1968, the Universal Fellowship of Metropolitan Community Churches now has more than 300 churches worldwide; in Britain it has branches in London, Manchester and Bournemouth.

The Unitarian Church tends to have liberal views of single-sex unions, although the views of individual ministers may differ. Also, there are some sympathetic clergy who may offer a service of blessing which may be arranged through the Lesbian and Gay Christian Movement.

Many Pagan and Humanist celebrants will also be willing to perform a marriage ceremony, the content of which may be decided between you. This will allow you to write your own vows of commitment to each other, creating a very personal celebration of your union.

For inspiration on the design of your ceremony, there are various books on the market that can assist:

- *The marriage of likeness: Same-sex unions* by John Boswell (HarperCollins, 1995)
- *Ceremonies of the heart (An anthology of lesbian unions)* by Beccy Butler (Seal Press, 1990)
- *Sharing the future: a practical guide to non-religious wedding ceremonies* by Jane Wynne Wilson (The British Humanist Society, 1996).

Even so, you should remember that no matter what ceremony you arrange, and no matter where it takes place, it will not be recognized as a legal marriage in the UK. It has recently become possible however, for same-sex couples to register their relationship. This does not convey the full range of rights enjoyed by married couples but it will, nevertheless, allow partners some entitlements in law. Check with the local registrar.

Unitarian

Most religious denominations view marriage as a holy sacrament, recognized by God; Unitarians view marriage as a decision made by two individuals in relation to their own spiritual views, and as a freely chosen act of commitment rather than an act of conformity.

The Unitarian Church welcomes people from different faiths or those who have been previously divorced, and if you are having difficulty finding a church that will marry you due to your particular circumstances, providing you are considered to have thought seriously about the commitment that you are to make, you will be welcomed.

Although the service itself must contain the legal words required, the rest of the service is completely individual to you, and may be arranged between you and the minister. You will be free to choose any style of language, readings, prayers, music and vows; you can adopt aspects of different religions and other cultural traditions.

A Unitarian minister will be able to perform the ceremony at any building registered for solemnization of weddings. However, if you wish to hold your wedding elsewhere, Unitarian ministers are generally happy to oblige, as long as you have a separate civil ceremony in advance.

General

If you are of different faiths, there may be difficulties when deciding on the type of wedding you want in order to keep both families happy. Just remember that this is only one day of your lives, and that what you want is most important. There are ways to compromise in almost every situation – talk to each other and to your families, who probably really only have your best interests at heart.

It may be possible to have two ceremonies, one of each faith; and to combine elements from each faith. Often the solution is to have two very distinct reception celebrations so that aspects of each faith and culture can be celebrated.

Register office

If the wedding is held at a register office, the ceremony will be much shorter than that in a church, but it can, and should, be just as meaningful and special. Many register office brides feel it inappropriate to wear a traditional wedding gown, or have attendants and music and so on, but this is a matter of custom, rather than because of any restrictions placed on registrars, their offices or those choosing to marry there.

It is true that many register offices are less than beautiful to look at but churches, too, can often seem cold and unfriendly, especially on a winter's day when the heating system shows all its inadequacies! Nevertheless, most register offices are pleasant places and staff will generally be warm and welcoming.

Before the ceremony

Preparations for the day will follow the same sort of pattern as for a church wedding but the ceremony itself is rather different. Generally, a register office wedding tends to be smaller, and more relaxed, than the church equivalent and it is likely that there will be few attendants, perhaps only one each for the bride and groom. Alternatively, the bride and groom may travel to the register office together, although the superstitious may find this quite beyond the pale!

Even though there may be no attendants to whom tasks can be delegated, someone will still need to make sure that the cake is safely at the reception, along with any gifts that are to be displayed, that flowers are delivered to the right place in plenty of time, and so on. Without the several pairs of willing hands normally supplied by attendants, the bride and her parents will need to find other ways of ensuring that last-minute tasks are completed properly, perhaps by pressing the bride's siblings into service (if she has them) or co-opting close friends.

Register offices have waiting areas where guests gather until it is time for the ceremony to begin. Since the ceremony is short, and register offices are sometimes quite busy, there may very well be two or more waiting areas, so that different bridal parties don't inconvenience each other. The way out of the office is often separated from the entrance for the same reason.

The ceremony

When the bride arrives, whether she is alone or with members of her family or friends, she can usually expect a warm welcome from the guests already congregated, often with hugs and kisses all round, something not possible in the more formal atmosphere of a church. The groom may also be there or he may already have been ushered into the marriage room to await her arrival.

The registrar's assistant will let everyone know when it is time to go through to the marriage room. The bride should wait a moment or two, then enter the room by herself, or on the arm of her father or appointed friend, and walk to the registrar's table where the groom awaits her. The room will not have an aisle, or altar, but the bride will walk through the centre, or down the side, of rows of seats occupied by her guests.

The registrar begins by welcoming the guests and saying a few words about the ceremony before asking the couple to exchange their vows and rings. When the short ceremony is over the newly-weds are invited to be seated while the Registrar supervises the signing of the register and copies the entry onto the Marriage Certificate which is given to the couple.

Photography and video

Registrars have the same concerns about photography and video recordings in the marriage room as ministers do for inside a church. Even though there are no religious considerations here, flash guns and the sound of cameras can be distracting so someone, preferably the best man, should be asked to tell guests carrying cameras whether there are restrictions on use. This is best done while guests are in the waiting area, before being shown into the marriage room.

Outside the office after the ceremony, there will be photographs and so on, exactly the same as at a church wedding. There is, however, a stronger possibility that a second location will be needed for photographs because many register offices open directly onto the street.

Second marriages

If the bride, or groom, or both, are marrying for the second time, there may very well be significant differences in how preparations, and the ceremony itself, are arranged.

For example, it is more likely that the bride and groom will have made all the arrangements and are paying for everything. Children from the couple's previous relationships may be present at the ceremony and there may be far less involvement from the couple's own parents, or even none at all.

Whatever arrangements the couple wish to make, whether for a small ceremony with only witnesses present, or an extravagant day's celebrations on a par with the classic formal church wedding, the choice is wide and entirely up to them.

06

design your
own ceremony

Designing your own ceremony may seem a daunting task. To begin with, you must decide upon the type of wedding that you want. Do you want a large, traditional wedding surrounded by family and friends, or a small ceremony attended by just a few people who are special to you? Your wedding may be your first, or it may involve bringing two existing families together to share your lives with each other's children. Unfortunately, finance may also have something to do with the size of the wedding that you are able to have.

The first things to consider are:

- the size of wedding that you want
- whether the ceremony is to be religious or civil
- the date and the time of day that you wish to marry
- the general theme for the day if you wish to do something a little different.

Once these decisions have been made, you can begin to develop an overall view of how you would like your wedding to proceed.

Firstly, obtain a copy of a standard wedding service applicable to your faith, or a copy of the civil marriage service. This will soon give you a basis from which to commence, and show you where you may insert your personalized music, promises, etc. Your minister or registrar will also be able to help with ideas and suggestions on where to look for inspiration.

Personalizing your own ceremony can be achieved through various aspects of the service:

- music
- hymns
- the service itself and the promises made
- clothing
- flowers
- transport
- rings
- cakes
- location.

You may wish to introduce certain elements of traditional custom and symbols of love, commitment and marriage – or elements from other cultures.

Music and hymns

The first area into which you can bring your own style is via the music chosen for:

- the period prior to the bride's arrival
- the processional (going in)

- during the service
- during the signing of the register, and
- the recessional (going out).

In the church or other venue you could consider using:

- a choir
- a piper
- a harpist
- a string quartet

- a soloist
- your favourite taped music
- a jazz ensemble.

If you have friends who play a musical instrument, such as a clarinet or guitar, they would probably feel honoured to be asked to play at your wedding. Strings or woodwind instruments could provide a classical touch, whilst a saxophone or even a steel band would provide a more contemporary feel to the service. This arrangement would be ideal for entertaining guests whilst the register is being signed.

Taped music is a good option for the processional and recessional parts of the service. Equipment may be hired and brought into the church if their own sound equipment is inadequate. You could appoint a reliable usher to take charge of the equipment and music.

If you are considering a religious ceremony, the music you choose should be appropriate to other surroundings, and possibly have some religious connection. If you decide to use the resident organist in a church, they will generally have a wide repertoire from which to choose.

Music played at civil ceremonies, either at the register office or other licensed venue should be entirely secular.

Generally speaking, the music for the processional should be slower in order that everyone can get a good look at the bride – and she can show off her dress! The recessional should have a more up-beat tempo, reflecting the happiness of the occasion. If you are to have hymns in the service, it is a good idea to choose ones that everyone knows, with a rousing chorus.

Music for the reception can also be chosen to suit your tastes. For example, you could choose any of the above to accompany the meal at the reception; you may wish to have walk-about musicians, such as a jazz trio, or a minstrel if you are having cocktails or drinks on arrival at the reception venue. Music later on in the evening could consist of either a disco or band specifically chosen to play music of your favourite era.

The service

In the Anglican Church, you may be offered the traditional service from the Book of Common Prayer, or the more usual service from the 'Alternative Service Book'.

Many Non-conformist churches have no set marriage service, and they offer something similar to the Anglican Church. Individual churches may have some guidelines that will provide you with a basic structure to the ceremony, but will be quite happy to assist you in the construction of a service to suit your personal circumstances. As long as the service fulfils the basic legal requirement, includes a statement about marriage and is approved by the minister, you are free to develop a service that reflects your personalities and style.

Customs and symbols of love, commitment and marriage

You are probably familiar with the saying about the bride's clothing that goes: 'Something old, something new, something borrowed, something blue. And a silver sixpence in your shoe.' The meaning of this is as follows.

- Something old has traditionally been an old garter (which is considered to be good luck), family jewellery or accessories from past family weddings.
- Something blue comes from an old Israeli tradition where the bride wears a blue ribbon as a symbol of her fidelity.
- The bride placing a coin in her shoe on her wedding day is said to bring wealth. If she chooses to follow this tradition, she would be wisest to stick it to the bottom of the shoe so that she doesn't end up limping by the end of the day!

Rings

The giving of rings is an ancient custom, and many people see their ring as a symbol of the promises made during their wedding. Rings need not necessarily be made of precious metal, and, indeed, you do not have to wear one at all. You could choose to have something other than a traditional gold band, choosing a ring with stones, made from a non-precious metal or even a ring pull from a can!

The custom of giving diamond engagement rings goes back to the fifteenth century, although the giving of rings originated in Roman times.

If the bride chooses to have a wedding ring with stones, she may wish to choose one with her birthstone, or a stone for its symbolism. The symbolism of various stones is described below.

Month	Birthstone	Meaning
January	Garnet	Constancy
February	Amethyst	Sincerity
March	Bloodstone	Courage
April	Diamond	Innocence
May	Emerald	Success
June	Pearl	Purity
July	Ruby	Love and contentment
August	Sardonyx	Married bliss
September	Sapphire	Wisdom
October	Opal	Hope
November	Topaz	Fidelity
December	Turquoise	Harmony

The bride may even wish to wear a REGARD ring (Ruby, emerald, garnet, amethyst, ruby, diamond). Although this is more commonly given as an eternity ring, there is no reason for it not to be given as a wedding ring – particularly if the bride does not have an engagement ring. If she chooses a ring with stones it would be a good idea to get the security of the stones checked on a regular basis as they may work loose if she wears the ring constantly.

The plain gold band style of wedding ring symbolizes eternity and the cycle of life. An alternative to a plain gold band may be a 'love ring' which became fashionable in the eighteenth century. It was made of interconnecting hoops which were held together by clasped hands enclosing a central heart. The rings are inseparable.

Some cultures do not exchange rings, but use other symbols as part of their marriage ceremony.

Money

There is an old Irish tradition whereby the bride and groom exchange silver and gold. This may be in the form of coins or jewellery, and is generally given after the ring.

Indian couples have bank notes pinned to their costumes by guests as a symbol of prosperity.

In Italy, the bride carries a *busta* or wedding bag, which is used to carry gifts of money. This dates back to Roman times.

Guests of a Greek wedding traditionally pin bank notes to the bride's dress.

Candles

Candles are used in several ceremonies – they may be used to show that the couple are two individuals becoming one, to light their paths as their new relationship comes into existence or as light being shared amongst those present at the ceremony.

Candles can be included in any floral decoration at the venue so that the couple may light them at the appropriate time.

In the United States the United Baptist Church Minister holds a three-stemmed candlestick. The two candles on the outside are lit to symbolize the two lives of the couple as they currently are; the centre candle is then lit to symbolize their lives as one together.

Flowers

Flora was the Roman Goddess of Spring, the vine, fruit, flowers and grain – and she symbolized fertility.

The placing of flower garlands around the couples' necks is common in some cultures. This could be introduced into your ceremony, particularly for a blessing in a garden or in a marquee. Alternatively, the couple could exchange a single flower as a symbol of their exchange of love.

In Hindu ceremonies, rose petals are thrown in front of the couple by their attendants during the recessional. Red and white rose petals were thrown in Saxon times to represent the union of passion and purity; this was the origin of confetti.

Flowers are an important part of the decoration for the ceremony venue, and for bouquets and posies. The bride can select what she wishes to say to her partner with her choice of flowers using the Victorian language of flowers. She could choose a bouquet to symbolize her feelings, and described opposite.

Flower	Meaning
Apple Blossom	Good fortune
Camellia	Gratitude/loveliness
Carnation	Fascination, love, betrothal
Chrysanthemum – white	Truth
Chrysanthemum – red	I love you/sharing
Cyclamen	Shyness, voluptuousness
Daffodil	Regard
Daisy	Innocence
Fern	Fascination/sincerity
Forget-me-not	True love
Gardenia	Joy
Heather	Good luck
Heliotrope	Devotion/faithfulness
Honeysuckle	Generosity/devotion
Hyacinth	Loveliness
Iris	Flame/burning love
Ivy	Good luck, eternal fidelity, marriage
Ivy geranium	Marriage
Japonica – white	Loveliness
Jasmine	Grace
Larkspur	Fickleness
Lemon blossom	Fidelity in love
Lily	Majesty/purity/modesty
Lily of the Valley	Happiness, return of happiness
Mimosa	Sensitivity
Myrtle	Love
Narcissus	Vanity
Orange Blossom	Chastity, virginity
Orchid	Beauty, perfection
Pansy	Thoughtfulness, remembrance, love

Pink	Boldness
Rose – red	Love, beauty, happiness
Rose – white	Purity, virginity, charm, secrecy
Rose – yellow	Remembrance
Snowdrop	Hope
Sweetpea	Pleasure
Tulip	Love
Veronica	Fidelity
Violet	Faithfulness

Above all other, the flower that has the greatest symbolism in many different cultures is the rose. It has come to represent youth, purity, perfection, earthly love and rebirth. Its essence is used to make love potions, cosmetics, teas and perfumes.

Canopies and banners

Several ethnic groups (Jewish, Hindu, Chinese) use canopies or banners over the couple during their wedding ceremony. Such canopies can be hired or made by specialist companies in London. If you are able to find a photograph in a wedding magazine of the type of floral canopy you would like, any good florist should be happy to tackle the job for you.

Confetti

Confetti throwing comes from an old Eastern tradition where rice was thrown. Rice is a symbol of fertility and was thrown so that the couple may be blessed with children. If you decide that rice should be thrown at your wedding (which is, of course, biodegradable and possibly more acceptable at venues which do not like traditional confetti), ask your guests to throw it high in the air and in small handfuls! It would not help to be blinded by a stray piece of rice on your wedding day!

The cake

The tradition of serving a wedding cake also dates from Roman times. The bride and groom cut the first slice together to show their lifelong devotion and harmony. Sharing the cake with their guests represents the union of two families.

Eating together is considered an important part of the marriage ceremony in many cultures; indeed, in Ancient Rome a marriage was not considered legally binding until the couple had shared bread together.

The cake may be decorated with symbols, such as:

- horse shoes – representing good luck
- silver bells – warding off evil spirits
- flowers made of icing – representing the flower symbols mentioned above
- bride and groom – on top of the cake representing their unity.

If you wish to have something a little more personal, there are many forms of cake that can be chosen to fit in with your theme and your own individual taste. Many people do not like the traditional fruit cake, so you may wish to choose a more popular alternative, such as:

- dark chocolate chip
- white chocolate
- orange
- cherry
- lemon
- carrot
- coffee
- vanilla madeira
- chocolate and orange
- chocolate and walnut
- rum and raisin
- ginger
- light fruit.

You may wish to choose a different cake for each tier to offer as an alternative to your guests.

There are many styles to choose from, such as:

- round, square, hexagonal, oval, heart-shaped tiers or single layers
- cakes to look like a pile of parcels
- a cake to look like your house
- if the bride wishes to be a princess like Cinderella, a cake in the shape of a pumpkin carriage, or a fairy castle
- if you are a vintage car fanatic, a cake shaped like your favourite car

- a cake decorated with flowers, either fresh or sugar, matching the bride's bouquet
- if you travel a great deal, a cake 'painted' with areas of the world that you have visited
- a cake in the shape of a bride and groom.

There are even companies that produce chocolate cakes with 100 per cent chocolate decoration in both traditional and modern style. These may take the form of a three-tier cake, with dark chocolate icing and red roses cascading from the top; white chocolate decorated with angels or flowers; or bright-red coloured chocolate with vibrant chocolate fruits decorating the sides.

Decide upon your theme, and find a good cake specialist that can accommodate you so that the style of the cake directly reflects the theme of wedding chosen. You could take inspiration from films, fashion, interior design, magazines, and books. Icing can be made to hang into swags, drapes and bows as well as into flowers and ribbons.

Another alternative to the traditional cake is the French wedding cake, called the *croquembouche* – crunch in the mouth! It is usually made of a pyramid of choux buns, filled with a flavoured cream and covered in caramel, peanut brittle and spun sugar. The cake needs to be served very fresh, and as it requires such skill to construct, it is best to ask an authentic French baker to make it. Although the ingredients are not as expensive as a traditional fruit cake, there is a great deal of skill in making a tower of profiteroles a metre high to serve 100 people! Also, you do not 'cut' the cake – you knock at it with a small hammer to break the crisp outer coating to allow the buns to be separated. They then need to be served on a plate with a fork as they are very sticky. This option is a good idea for those on a budget as they can serve the *croquembouche* as the dessert as well as the wedding cake; however, you will not be able to send pieces to those not able to attend the reception.

Another way to combine dessert and wedding cake is to follow the Italian tradition of a cassata as a wedding cake. This is a delicious ice-cream bombe, layered with sponge and set with fruits and nuts. Obviously, an ice-cream wedding cake cannot be on display throughout the reception, but may be brought out in splendour at the appropriate time for the bride and groom to cut.

Colour

Brides in the United Kingdom traditionally get married in white. However, she could choose another colour if she is getting married for the second time, or wishes to marry abroad. The colour in which the bride is married is surrounded in superstition, as described below.

- White – you've chosen all right
- Blue – your love is true
- Pearl – you'll live in a whirl
- Brown – you'll live out of town
- Red – you will wish yourself dead!
- Yellow – you're ashamed of your fellow
- Green – you're ashamed to be seen (unless you're Irish, when it's lucky!)
- Pink – your fortunes will sink
- Grey – you'll live far away
- Black – you'll wish yourself back.

White has only been a relatively modern choice for brides, with Queen Victoria choosing the first white wedding dress when she married Prince Albert. Prior to that time, most royal brides wore silver, and in Roman times, brides wore yellow.

Oriental brides frequently wear bright colours, and, in particular, Chinese brides consider red to be the luckiest colour of all. In India, the bride's red sari stands for fertility. The couple may be given garlands of roses to represent happiness and beauty.

Sharing bread and wine

If you are getting married in church, particularly into the Catholic faith, a communion service may be held as part of the wedding itself. If this is not appropriate to the service that you are planning, sharing bread and wine is a good alternative; it is an ancient symbol of trust and peace between people.

Traditional customs of ethnic groups

If you and/or your partner are from different ethnic backgrounds, or have strong links with an ethnic group, you may like to consider adopting some of the traditional customs from that culture. Alternatively, you may have travelled and liked the style of living in another country, or even got engaged abroad and want to include some of that country's traditional customs in your ceremony. The list below is by no means exhaustive, but does give you a taste of the traditions of various religions and cultures around the world. You may choose to encompass some of these traditions into your own wedding ceremony.

If you decide to adopt any of these customs, you should be able to develop them into an overall theme for your wedding that is entirely personal to you.

African

The bride wears her hair braided over her face to symbolize her modesty. Guests generally wear traditional African robes, which are colourful and highly decorative.

The ceremony includes 'jumping the broom'. This involves the couple, jumping together, over a broom decorated with flowers, which symbolizes them jumping into domestic bliss! Wine is poured on the ground as a symbol of liberation. Guests are entertained at the wedding party by drums and Congo music – with much dancing.

American Indian

The Navajo is the largest American-Indian ethnic group. Their ceremonies are usually held in the evening, facing east, which is considered to be the direction of the future. Brides wear a woven dress in symbolic colours: white for the east; blue for the south; yellow for the west and black for the north. A silver colcho belt and silver and turquoise jewellery are worn. These protect the couple by acting as a shield against illness, bad fortune, hunger, etc.

During the ceremony, white and yellow cornmeal are mixed to make a corn mush which is placed in the Navajo wedding basket. The white symbolizes the male, and the yellow symbolizes the female, and they are joined together in the wedding basket. The dish is shared between the couple during the ceremony to depict their bond in marriage.

Arabic

As in India (see below), the bride is decorated with hennaed patterns. She wears a caftan that is highly decorated. The women perform a 'wedding wail'; this is mourning the loss of the bride to her new family.

Receptions are segregated by sex; Middle-Eastern food is served. Music will be Arabic, performed on pigskin drums, accompanied by singers and rhythmic dancers.

Cajun (Deep South, USA)

After the ceremony there is a great deal of partying, commencing with a jazzy wedding march of all the guests following the bride and groom, dancing and waving colourful handkerchiefs. Single women dance on upturned washtubs to attract the attention of potential suitors.

At the bride's home, traditional foods such as boudin sausage, jambalaya and spicy peppers will be served. Guests often bring hundreds of home-made cakes – there may even be a room set aside as a 'cake room' to accommodate them!

Caribbean

Calypso music, steel drums and guitars entertain the couple and guests during and after the ceremony. A traditional wedding cake, which is extremely rich and dark, is served; it is made with candied fruits and steeped in rum. The cake can be made into various shapes, such as houses or gardens, etc. In some areas, couples plant a tree for prosperity.

Chinese

At Chinese weddings, a canopy is used for the couple to marry under, which often takes the form of an umbrella. The wedding honours the couple's parents and elders in a ceremony of obligation.

The traditional colours of happiness, good luck and wealth are worn – red, green and gold; clothing, decorations, invitations and wrapped gifts may also be in all these colours. 'Lucky money' is presented in red envelopes.

During the celebrations, the bride typically changes her clothing as many as three times. As the couple leave the reception, firecrackers are placed in their paths to ward off evil spirits.

Czech

A male member of the family presents the bride to the groom before entering the church, and tells them to fulfil their duties to each other. The bridesmaids pin a sprig of rosemary to each guest as a symbol of fertility and long life.

During the ceremony, the bride's veil is removed, and replaced by an apron and a matron's bonnet, whilst the guests sing a traditional wedding song. After the ceremony their path is blocked as they leave the church (as in Germany); the couple's family and friends pay money to allow the couple to pass.

Traditional foods, such as sauerkraut, sausage, apple strudel and fruit-filled rolls (*kolaches*) are served to guests at the reception.

Filipino

At the celebration, guests and family of the couple dance with them whilst pinning money to their clothes.

At the feast, traditional foods such as roast hog will be served. A giant canopy of flowers in the shape of a bell will be situated over the couple during the reception. At the end of the festivities the couple will pull ribbons to release two doves which have been trapped in the bell, to symbolize their everlasting love for each other.

Finnish

Finnish brides have a 'hope chest', similar to French brides (see below).

After the ceremony, the couple plant Lily of the Valley pips in their garden; when the flowers come up each year, this symbolizes the renewal of their love for each other.

French

The bride has a hope chest ('wedding armoire') for her trousseau, which is handcarved with symbols of wealth and prosperity.

Traditionally, everything is white – the dress, the flowers and the decorations. Laurel leaves are thrown before the couple as they leave the church. At the reception, the couple shares a drink from a wedding cup.

After the wedding, the couple leave for their first night together, and are often interrupted by the noise of pots being bashed together – the groom is supposed to invite the mischief-makers in for refreshments!

German

The celebrations begin the night before the actual ceremony, with a wedding eve party (*polterabend*), with much plate smashing.

The bride is carried to church in a horse-drawn carriage, led by black horses. After the ceremony, the couple are prevented from leaving the church by red ribbons and garlands which are used to block their exit; they must bargain for their exit either with money, or the promise of a party. They are then free to make their way to their reception party in the horse-drawn carriage.

The reception meal is a generous feast, accompanied by spiced wine and beer. Marzipan confectionery is served at the end of the meal. After the reception, guests are invited to the couple's home to inspect the house, the furnishings and the gifts that they have been given. The couple entertain their guests at home.

Greek

Historically, the Roman Empire conquered Greece; thus some Greek traditions have been adopted from Italy (see the section below on Italy). For example, 'favours' wrapped in tulle are given to the guests at the reception, as they are in Italy. However, instead of being presented by the bride, they are selected and paid for by the sponsor of the wedding. Also, at the reception, guests participate in a traditional circle dance while holding handkerchiefs, known as the *kalamantiano*.

During the ceremony, a chanter urges the groom to honour his bride, and the bride taps the groom's foot to emphasize the point. The reception meal includes many Greek foods that are now well known to us, such as stuffed vine leaves and lamb kebabs, accompanied by Greek wine.

Indian

At Hindu weddings, a canopy is used again, generally made from flowers that are strung from either an archway or a metal framework with four legs. The whole platform upon which the couple stands is decorated with the same flowers.

The bride will wear red or magenta, which is the colour of celebration and happiness. Her hands and feet are intricately painted with henna – without this, the bride's appearance would be incomplete. Patterns used are very lace-like, and considered auspicious. Her face is decorated, which is the privilege of married women. The groom may wear a white suit made of brocade, with a turban, and carry a sword. He may wear a veil of flowers over his face and turban on his way to the ceremony. Garlands of white flowers are given to welcome family members, and honour their presence.

The ceremony is generally carried out at the bride's home. The groom and his family will form a procession, together with wedding guests, to the house. The family presents money in baskets to the couple at the ceremony.

Irish

Traditionally, the Irish wedding ring has the design of two hands holding a heart with a crown above; the two hands are worn facing inwards, called the 'Claddagh'. The couple are showered with flower petals as they leave the church. At the reception, the groom is lifted in a chair ('jaunting car') to present him as a married man. At the reception, the feast would include ham and cabbage.

Italian

Italian brides traditionally carry a small bag (*busta*) which is used to hold any gifts of money that are presented to them during the day. Money is given by guests to ensure wealth during the bride's marriage.

Bridal parties are large (as are most Italian families!), and wedding feasts sumptuous and extravagant. A special Italian cake is served at the end of the feast, which is light and dotted with dried crystallized fruits.

Bridal favours (*bomboniere*) originate from Italy – they are traditionally a decorated bag containing five sugared almonds, representing health, wealth, happiness, long life and fertility. They are presented by the bride (or are left beside place settings at the reception) as a thank you to guests for attending the wedding ceremony.

During the reception, guests are entertained by participating in the traditional wedding circle dance, the Tarantella.

Japanese

Although the Japanese consider red to be a lucky, joyous colour, this is only used to decorate the surroundings of the celebration. The bride herself is usually dressed in a white jacquard silk kimono, decorated with the groom's family crest. She also wears a wedding wig, and heavily jewelled ornaments. The bride will change from her wedding outfit for the banquet.

The reception feast includes red rice, kelp and sea bream (a ceremonial fish of happiness), accompanied by rice wines. Toasts, speeches and stories about the couple are told by elder members of the families and honoured guests to entertain them. Decorations will include many candles.

Jewish

Prior to the wedding ceremony, the bride attends the *mikva*, or traditional ritual bath. This marks her transition from one life into another.

The ceremony itself takes place under a *chuppah* which is made of fabric, supported on four poles. It is used to represent the home in which the bridal couple are setting up together, and as a mark of respect. The *chuppah* may be embroidered, appliquéd or decorated with flowers and is held over the couple's heads during the ceremony. If the couple choose to make their own *chuppah*, the fabric, if suitably decorated, may be hung as a wall-hanging in their home after the wedding.

A marriage contract, often extremely artistic, is presented to the couple and is displayed after the wedding in the couple's home.

At the reception after the end of the ceremony, the groom stamps on a glass. Kosher-style food is served (nor pork or shellfish, and meat and dairy products are not served at the same meal). Guests participate in the traditional dance, the *hora*, after the meal.

Lithuanian

On their way to the ceremony, the couple pass under a bridge of embroidered sashes. After the ceremony, the couple receives bread, salt, wine and honey from their parents to symbolize the elements of their lives together.

Mexican

Before the ceremony, the parents of the couple bless them as they leave home. The ceremony is conducted in Spanish, with the couple kneeling on their special 'kneeling pillow'. Godparents have special roles in the ceremony.

During the ceremony, a lasso is tied around the couple in a figure of eight, to symbolize their being tied together.

The groom presents 13 gold coins to the bride as a symbol of his commitment to her and his support for her. These are contained in a small chest (*arras*) made of gold symbolizing wealth and strength, which is blessed during the service.

At the banquet, traditional foods of rice, beans, tortilla dishes, beef and chicken are served. The wedding party is entertained with guitar music and songs.

Polish

Before the ceremony, the bridesmaids undo the bride's maidenly braids. It is customary to wear a wreath of Laurel.

Children hold ropes or chains in front of the couple to bar their way; the best man has to pay them off. The couple are then greeted by their parents, and welcomed with bread and salt which represent prosperity and bitterness.

At the reception, the guests give the couple money, and the bride gives the guests gifts in return. During the reception, the bride is subjected to a mock kidnap. Traditional foods such as roasts, pickled herrings, noodles and a special wedding bread in the shape of flowers, animals or pinecones are eaten. Music to entertain guests includes polkas and mazurkas.

Russian

During the reception, after the toasts are made, champagne glasses are thrown to the floor. If they break, the couple can expect a life filled with happiness.

On leaving the reception, couples tie toys to their wedding car. If they tie a teddy to it, they wish their first born to be a boy; if they tie on a doll, they wish it to be a girl.

Scandinavian

The bride wears a jewelled wedding crown (vasa crown) which symbolizes her innocence.

Horns and fiddlers accompany the couple as they make their way to the church, and 'care cloths' are held over the couple to protect them from evil spirits as they make their vows and receive their final blessings.

The wedding feast may well be a traditional smorgasbord, which is a tempting array of hot and cold foods, arranged on platters. The food is accompanied by, and toasts are made with, a specially brewed beer called *skoal*. The Swedish wedding cake is more bread-like than cake, and is called *brundlaupskling*.

Slavic

Before the bride leaves home for the wedding ceremony, her mother washes the steps of her home to symbolize the washing away of the bride's old life, and the beginning of a new one. A traditional circle dance (the *horo*) is performed at the reception. A bread-like wedding cake is served to guests (a *koluk*).

Slovak

As in Czech ceremonies, the guests pin live sprigs of rosemary onto their lapels.

The bride wears a beautifully embroidered wedding shawl, and a wedding headdress. During the ceremony the headdress is removed, and replaced by a cap made from crochet (a *cepec*) – this is known as the 'capping ceremony'.

At the reception, poppyseed pastries are traditionally served. Music will include polkas and waltzes, and guests dance the *csardas*, a traditional dance.

Ukrainian

Prior to the service, the couple's parents present them with religious icons. Included in the ceremony is the hanging of an effigy of the matchmaker. A mock 'capture' of the bride is re-enacted at the reception.

Vietnamese

The bride wears pink or red as a sign of her happiness. Flowers and decorations are also pink or red. The groom's family offer clothes, money and jewellery to the bride, to welcome her to their family.

The celebration itself generally consists of two parties, one given by the groom's parents and one by the bride's. During the preparation for the celebration and during the celebration itself, it is said to be unlucky if anyone breaks a glass or dish – if something is broken it is said to be a bad omen and may lead to the break-up of the marriage.

The commencement of the ceremony

If you have been living together for some time, or are an older couple, the bride may not wish to be 'given away'. If this is the case, there is no reason why she should not walk down the aisle on her own, or with a 'best woman'.

The bride may wish to be met at the door of the church by her groom, and walk together down the aisle. This would also be appropriate if, as a couple, you have children. They could stand with their father at the door waiting for the bride to arrive; you could then all proceed down the aisle together as a family unit to declare your commitment to each other as a family as well as a couple.

Alternatively, if the bride has no close male member of the family, she may choose to have her mother, older sister or aunt take on the task of giving her away.

Today, the role of the best man is not always taken by a male; there is no reason why the 'best man' should not be a woman. Likewise, ushers need not be men, but may be female family members.

Vows

Generally speaking, if you are marrying in the Church of England or the Catholic Church, you will have very little opportunity to alter the actual words of the ceremony, as they are obligatory and must stand as written. You may choose to obey or not, and you may choose to 'respect' instead of 'honour' but this is the only area in which vows may be altered as they are part of the legal marriage contract. Readings and hymns are the areas in which you stamp your own mark.

In the standard service, the vows take place towards the beginning of the ceremony, when nobody has really had the chance to settle down. You may wish to introduce an extra hymn or reading at the beginning of the service in order that the vows take place in the middle of the ceremony to give them greater focus.

If you are marrying in another faith, you will have much greater freedom to write your own ceremony. Once the legal part of the ceremony is out of the way, how you state your vows, what you add or subtract is, with the minister's approval, up to you. More forward-looking Anglican and Catholic ministers may also be willing to assist you in writing your vows to conform to their religious ceremonies.

The vows in the modern wedding service as as follows:

I, X, take you, Y, to be my wife,
to have and to hold
from this day forward;
for better, for worse,
for richer, for poorer,
in sickness and in health
to love and to cherish*
till death us do part,
according to God's holy law;
and this is my solemn vow.

*this may be altered to read 'to love, cherish and worship' for the groom, and 'to love, cherish and obey' for the bride.

After blessing the ring(s), the minister hands the bride's ring to the groom, who says:

I give you this ring
as a sign of marriage.
With my body I honour you,
all that I am I give to you,
and all that I have I share with you,
within the love of God,
Father, Son and Holy Spirit

If the groom is to receive a ring, the bride repeats the wording above. If not, the bride says:

I receive this ring
as a sign of our marriage ... [and continues as above].

You may wish to write your own vows to each other based on the above wording. These may be written in more informal, everyday language, such as:

I, *X*, take you *Y*, to be my husband,
my one true partner for life,
from this moment forward;
for the good times, and when times get tough,
in times of prosperity, and in times of poverty
in times of good health, and in times of sickness and grief,
whilst we are young and when we grow old;
to love, support and respect you,
to encourage you for the rest of my life,
with God's help, this is my promise to you.

Inspiration for vows may come from a variety of sources:

- the Bible (See Old Testament book of Ruth, Chapter 1 vs. 16 and 17 – see below)
- poetry
- music
- literature
- other faiths
- other countries.

You might wish to incorporate your own version of Ruth's promise to Naomi (from the Bible):

I will not leave you, I will go with you.
Wherever you go, I will go,
wherever you live, I will live.
Your people will be my people,
and your God will be my God.
Wherever you die, I will die, and that is where I will be buried.
May the Lord's worst punishment come upon me if I let anything but death separate me from you.

You may feel that this is a little strong for your promise, but it is stated here for inspirational purposes in order that you can develop your own version!

You could also bring in an element of your commitment to other projects as well as to each other, for example, if you are members of Amnesty International, you may wish to add a promise such as by both saying together:

We promise to do our best to oppose injustice and suffering wherever it may be encountered.

Alternatively, the traditional promises may be interwoven, such as:

Adrian:	I take you, Beverley,
Beverley:	I take you, Adrian,
Adrian:	to be my wife,
Beverley:	to be my husband,
Both:	from this day forward and forever.
Adrian:	For better or for worse,
Beverley:	in good times and when things get tough,
Adrian:	for richer and poorer,
Beverley:	in prosperity and poverty,
Adrian:	in sickness and in health,
Beverley:	whilst we are young, and when we are old.
Adrian:	To love, encourage and respect you,
Beverley:	to love, support and cherish you,
Both:	for the rest of our lives, with God's help, I promise.

Another way of personalizing your service, if marrying in church, is to write your own prayers, devoting yourselves to each other and asking for God's blessing.

In some marriage ceremonies, the congregation are asked to give their support to the couple during their lives together, and are invited to add their promise to the service. This could also be added during the prayers at the end of the ceremony:

> Do you, as friends of X and Y, promise to encourage and support them in their married lives together?
> We do.

This would make guests more a part of the actual ceremony, rather than just on-lookers.

Remember, a civil wedding ceremony must not include any passages that have a religious connotation. You can get around this by telling the registrar, beforehand, that you want to include passages taken from the Bible, a prayer book, the Koran or any other religious book or tract, and asking him or her to help you ensure that the legal part of the ceremony is sufficiently separated from your own additions.

Religious references aren't a problem if you're marrying in a church synagogue, temple or other meeting house, and the minister, priest, imam or other leader is amenable to your requests.

Your local library, or the internet, will help you locate suitable secular poetry and literature. The internet, especially, is overflowing with romance. Much of it is poor quality but there is plenty there for every taste, if you're willing to look through it all!

Involving children

If you already have children, it is a good idea to involve them in the wedding ceremony as the vows you are about to make affect their lives almost as much as they affect yours. Some churches actively encourage the participation of any children of the couple. Children may be involved by being participants in the wedding party, such as bridesmaids, pageboys or ushers. If they are old enough, they could act as witnesses to the marriage in either a church or civil wedding, but they would need to be mature to do so.

They may also be able to take part more actively in the service itself. They could enter the ceremony venue at the same time as their parents, and be with them during the wedding.

The wedding service of the United Reformed Church includes vows to be made by family members other than the couple, which involve them promising to support and encourage those getting married.

Alternatively, Hannah Ward and Jennifer Wild, in their book *Human Rites* (Mowbray) have included 'A ceremony for recognising children during the wedding ceremony'. Children are presented with a token of the shared bond which their parents have formed as a result of the marriage. After the vows made by the couple themselves, a reading could be given in praise for the blessing of the children. Prayers can also be said not only for the couple, but for them and their children as a family.

If your children are very young, give them a pot of bubbles! They can stand at the door of the ceremony venue as you depart and shower you with bubbles, as an alternative to confetti.

Enjoy your wedding!

If you wish to make your promises and vows personal to you – do so. Speaking to the registrar or minister who will preside over the wedding at the outset about your plans to design your own ceremony is likely to make them more receptive to the idea than being presented with it once all the 't's' are crossed and the 'i's' dotted. They have a wealth of experience, and can assist you in deciding what is and is not appropriate and will, generally speaking, be receptive to any customs or family traditions that you wish to introduce to the service.

The reception

Guests must enjoy the wedding, and share in a relaxed, happy atmosphere. No matter how informal your wedding is to be, unless you really object to this, a traditional receiving at the commencement of the reception is advisable. This gives you the opportunity to spend a couple of minutes with each guest in turn, making them feel important to your day. This does not have to be carried out in a formal line made up of the whole of the bridal party, with guests waiting in a queue; if drinks are served on arrival you will be able to drift amongst guests to say a few words.

The timing of the wedding is also important. It is best to arrange your wedding breakfast or buffet to coincide with regular meals in order that guests are ready to eat. If you are to continue into the evening with further friends joining the party later, a light snack may also be served towards the middle of the evening. The time of the ceremony should be arranged to fit in with your reception plans, and also with a mind to the distance that guests will need to travel.

General

The most important thing about your wedding day is that you enjoy it! You should try to share some of the responsibility of organizing the wedding by passing some jobs on to other members of the wedding party, reliable members of your family or by employing a wedding co-ordinator. There is a lot to think about, and, for example, passing to your sister or brother the simple job of addressing and sending off the invitations and monitoring replies will save a great deal of worry.

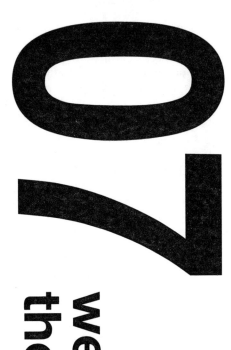

07

wedding themes

Period themes

Period themes for weddings are becoming more and more popular as people try to break away from the norm. Couples often choose a period theme because they share a special interest or affinity with that time in history. Sometimes the bride may just see or imagine 'the perfect dress', which may look out of place in a traditional setting. There are many costumiers and dressmakers that are able to hire or supply dresses to fit with a period theme; often a local dressmaker will be able to construct a good copy from a photograph or picture in a book if the bride is able to find something similar to her dream dress.

Inspiration for your period theme may come from television dramas, books, plays, or films. Often, weddings depicted in these are given a 'dream-like' quality, which can make a bride realize that she does not want an ordinary dress, with an ordinary ceremony, with ordinary music and reception fare.

If you feel that you were born in the wrong century or decade, go with that feeling and decide which part of history you would like to experience on your wedding day. The themes set out here will give you some idea of the extent to which you can give a period theme to your wedding, and how to capture the romance of the period, as well as providing you with a starting block for your imagination.

Celtic or Anglo-Saxon wedding

Although these eras are very distinct periods in history, many elements of lifestyles were similar and are combined for the purpose of this theme.

The Celts were probably the first iron-using tribes in Britain, and made the first bronze for music horns, cups, platters and jewellery. They lived in groups of circular huts, and the chieftains, their warriors and their priests, called druids, dominated life. A wedding theme based on Celtic life would be simply decorated, and would suit an outdoor, informal reception.

Ceremony and venue
If you wish to adopt a Celtic theme, remember that the Celts lived in the age just after Stonehenge was built. The sun, the moon and the stars were great influences on the lives of people at this time.

After a simple ceremony at a register office, you may choose to undergo a marriage agreement in a Celtic style – or use the Anglo-Saxon 'handfasting' ceremony (which represented their marriage agreement). An ideal venue would be on a high point in the countryside, possibly overlooking wooded surroundings. Permission may be obtainable from English Heritage or the National Trust to hold a ceremony at various monuments from this age throughout the country, such as Castlerigg Stone Circle in the Lake District. Most stone circles have open access, such as Ong Meg in Cumbria, Avebury in Wiltshire (which is even larger than the more famous Stonehenge) and many historic sites in Ireland. The landscape and ancient sites, such as old Celtic hill-forts in Scotland, would also be perfect venues for such a ceremony. You may even be able to obtain permission from tourist centres which have reconstructed Anglo-Saxon villages – these can be identified by contacting your local tourist information office.

If you do not have access locally to any venue that you consider suitable, you could consider constructing your own sacred space by planting a circle of trees or placing a circle of stones within which to celebrate your marriage – even within your own garden.

You will need a celebrant for the service – these can be contacted through the Pagan Federation (see Taking it further). You could choose to have a Celtic celebrant, or a druid or druidess to perform the ceremony.

There are various rituals that may be included within the ceremony, such as flower maidens sprinkling petals before the bride as she walks, a broom-jumping ritual, or music or poetry.

The basic Celtic ceremony involves using symbols of the four elements and the four directions: stone or crystal for north, candles for south, incense for east and water for west. Bread and wine are also used in the ceremony.

The celebrant creates a sacred space with flower petals, which follows the circle of life: birth, childhood, maturity and death. The symbols of the chalice, the bread, the wine and the rings are placed on their appropriate altars. The powers of nature are called upon to bless the couple. Poems, songs and blessings may be read.

The celebrant then performs a ceremony similar to that of the Christian communion with all the guests present, after which the couple exchange vows of commitment to each other and give each other rings as a symbol of their union.

This form of ceremony gives you ample opportunity to write your own poems or songs about your love for each other, to use music or musicians to enhance the enjoyment of the service, and to personalize your vows of commitment.

Clothing

Celtic brides did not cover their faces with veils, but did wear circlet-style headdresses or tiaras. They were based on knotwork designs, and did not generally contain precious stones. Alternatively, a circlet of wild flowers would be appropriate, such as daisies. Brides also wore simple necklaces in a single band of metal, similar to a choker.

The clothing worn would be of a simple tunic style, gathered into the waist with a sash or belt. They would have been dyed in natural colours from the flower and plant dyes that were made at the time. The Celts were able to weave patterns into their cloth for decorative purposes. For inspiration you may like to consult the film 'Braveheart' for ideas about a Celtic wedding.

You may like to consider a romantic alternative to a Celtic ceremony. If you choose the Anglo-Saxon wedding, a 'King Arthur's Court' setting could be appropriate, with Guinevere as inspiration for a bridal gown and headdress.

Transport

Transportation to the ceremony – whether in Celtic or Anglo-Saxon times – would have been on foot, with the bridal couple followed by family members. If you wish to arrive in greater style, a simple horse-drawn carriage or chariot may be hired.

Food

If the setting for the wedding is outside, an ideal option for food would be a barbecue buffet, consisting of either spit-roast or barbecued chicken, lots of wholegrain breads and simple salads, followed by forest fruits. Ideally this would be served on wooden or simple pottery platters and eaten with the fingers for an authentic feel.

Traditionally, eating would have taken place around a central fire, seated either on the ground, or on slatted wooden benches, possibly covered with furs or woven fabric.

To replicate this, it would be possible to have an open fire, and seat guests either on wooden pallets or on hay bales (which may be obtained from local farmers), covered with blankets.

Decoration

If the weather is not suitable for an outdoor wedding, the hire of a local hall or marquee may lend itself to transformation into a Celtic or early English settlement. Walls of traditional boundaries of the settlements and housing were made of wattle and daub, which may be adequately replicated inside a hall by securing woven fencing panels around the perimeter. Trees and large foliage plants may be hired to create a 'woodland' area where a ceremony may be conducted. A 'star' cloth may be hired from most marquee companies, which is a black cloth with small holes through which artificial light shines, making an effective star-lit background. Wooden benches, and wall-hangings and coverings of woven fabrics would enhance the decoration, along with large sections of tree trunk that may also be used for seating around the room.

Although it would be impossible to have an actual fire inside a building or marquee, a stone surround for a 'fire' could be constructed as a focal point, over which a large cauldron could be hung – possibly containing a punch to which people could help themselves!

Music and entertainment

After the ceremony and the meal, you will probably require some form of dancing. Although not strictly authentic, country/barn dancing could be appropriate, as most guests will be familiar with this. You might wish to bring in pipes, horns or accordions at this point to accompany the dancing, and someone to call the dance will be essential to keep everyone going in the right direction!

Seventeenth and eighteenth centuries

Wedding themes in this era have become very popular. The television dramatizations of the novels written by Jane Austen, such as *Pride and Prejudice* and *Sense and Sensibility* give a good insight into eighteenth-century life. Viewing of the BBC videos of those dramatizations is recommended so that you can get a feel for the era, and for the way in which a wedding was celebrated.

Inspiration may also be drawn for a country-style wedding from the paintings of the appropriate time – for example, the landscapes of Thomas Gainsborough.

Ceremony and venue

A traditional church service would have been very similar to that of today's traditional Book of Common Prayer service.

If you wish to have a civil ceremony, many fine mansions from this period have been turned into hotels, and are licensed. For example:

- Haughton Hall, Shifnal, Shropshire
- Eastwell Manor, Ashford, Kent
- Brandshatch Place, Fawkham, Kent
- The Close Hotel, Tetbury, Gloucestershire
- Bindon Country House Hotel and Restaurant, Wellington, Somerset
- The Kingston Estate, Totnes, Devon
- The Haycock, Peterborough, Cambridgeshire
- Theobalds Park, Cheshunt, Hertfordshire
- Bassetsbury Manor, High Wycombe, Buckinghamshire.

Poetry from the time could be chosen as readings for the ceremony, such as that written by William Wordsworth, Robert Burns and Lord Byron. Poetry of this time is written in a language that all can enjoy, and is appropriately romantic.

Clothing

Again, the TV dramatizations will give you good insight into the fashions of the time. Clothing such as this may be hired from theatrical hire companies. The dresses of the time are easy to wear – and walk in – and will remain comfortable during the day and on into the evening.

A veil or flowers pinned in the bride's hair would be appropriate to accompany the simple lines of the clothing of the time. It would also suit the hairstyles of the time, which tended to be long, and curled into ringlets. Other members of the bridal party may choose to wear mob caps (for smaller bridesmaids) or poke bonnets.

Carrying fans was popular at the time, and would make a suitable alternative to flowers for any member of the bridal party. Another alternative would be a parasol.

In the seventeenth century it was very fashionable to wear 'patches' on the face by way of make-up – such as hearts, circles, moons and stars. The decorative jewellery was actually to hide the marks left by diseases such as smallpox, but became the 'in' thing for the aristocracy!

The end of the eighteenth century saw the invention of the top hat; therefore, a hired morning suit with a frock coat would be appropriate for the groom, best man and other male members of the bridal party.

Transport

A horse and carriage is the obvious choice for a wedding of this period but bear in mind the time of year that you are to be married, and the number of your bridal party. There are a number of styles available from a single horse trap, to a coach and four. You should not have difficulty in finding a carriage to suit your requirements.

If you live too far from the church or ceremony venue to come all the way by coach and horses, you could arrange with a friend or colleague who lives close to the venue to pick up the coach from their home. This would involve leaving home in a car, changing to the horse and carriage, and swapping back again after the ceremony. A carriage ride is slow, and is really only suitable for short distances: you don't want to arrive at your reception to find that the party is over!

Food

The gentry of the seventeenth century were increasingly affluent, which resulted in a great deal of entertaining. Until this time, the food eaten was generally home-produced meat, game and grain which was roasted, boiled or baked as required – quantity was more important than quality. Meat would still have formed three-quarters of the food on the table. However, a wide variety of vegetables and salads were also served.

You might wish to choose a casserole such as Lancashire Hot Pot, chicken cooked in wine, or a roast or spit-roast meat, accompanied by vegetables and bread. Potatoes were still somewhat rare at this time.

The 'pudding' came into its own at this time, with many of the traditional English desserts originating from the seventeenth or eighteenth centuries. Many of these desserts are again popular today, and something such as bread and butter pudding, steamed puddings or syllabub would be appropriate to this theme.

To follow the traditions of the time, only two, or at most three, courses should be served. The major meat dishes should be served at the same time as the soup. Once the soup is finished, the serving dish should be replaced with an alternative vegetable dish. In the second course, a range of lighter meats and desserts should be served. If a third course is served, it should comprise fruit, sweetmeats and cheese. Diners help themselves to whatever they desire from a buffet that is served at individual tables.

With regard to serving the food, tables were first covered with a fine linen cloth. Silver and pewter tableware were still used, but the introduction of brightly coloured tableware was becoming common. Glassware was used for wine glasses, tumblers and desserts.

The most significant introduction to the tableware of the seventeenth century was the knife and fork. Until this time, food was generally eaten using the fingers, spoons and bread – nobility had used forks since the fourteenth century, but only for eating sweetmeats.

Decoration
Finding the right venue for a wedding with this kind of historical theme will solve most of the decorative problems. Flowers in large, brightly coloured pottery vases, and pottery, silver or carved wooden candlesticks would be appropriate table decorations. As most people will be serving themselves from their own 'buffet', it would be wise to keep table decoration to a minimum, allowing brightly coloured pottery plates already set out with food to decorate the tables.

If you have a large banqueting hall to decorate, pedestals of flowers would add impact and a softness to the room.

Music and entertainment
If you wish to adopt this theme, the use of a harpist before and during the ceremony would be a nice, individual touch. Alternatively, you could choose a string quartet to entertain guests during the signing of the register, or during the meal at your reception.

Dancing was very popular at this time, with large family gatherings and ceremonial balls. However, it is unlikely that your guests will have an in-depth knowledge of dances of the time, and you might wish to go for something a little more modern for the evening.

Other period themes

There are many more period themes to choose from and these include:

- Roman
- Medieval
- Tudor
- Victorian
- 1920s/1930s
- 1940s/1950s
- 1960s
- futuristic

- American Colonial
- British Raj
- Egyptian Pharoahs
- Australian Outback

Take care, and be sensitive, when you design your own wedding in a cultural theme. You could inadvertently give great offence to someone who might consider that you are trivializing their ethnicity and heritage.

Cultural themes

With increased freedom of movement across countries and continents, and emigration and business travel becoming ever more common, unions between individuals with differing backgrounds are now more the rule than the exception. To embrace the differences between the two of you, you may decide to have a wedding that encompasses aspects from different cultures – or even have two ceremonies. Acknowledging the differences between the two of you will not only celebrate your backgrounds, but also show respect for your parents, making them feel more at home with the wedding ceremony itself.

If you wish to embrace elements from your cultural background and design your own ceremony to reflect this, refer to Chapter 5 and Chapter 6. These cover the basic traditions and customs of many ethnic groups, and would be a good place to begin.

This section covers general perceptions of cultures, and although these may not be strictly accurate they do lend themselves well to a wedding theme. The basics of theming your reception are detailed – but with a little imagination, this can be carried through from the invitations to the ceremony, and on to the reception itself. The themes covered here are relaxed. It is intended that people move around and mix, rather than feel that they have to remain seated at their place as shown on a table plan and wait for the rituals of a standard reception.

Caribbean

Venue
For this theme you should try to create a tropical island paradise. Any venue would be suitable for this purpose, but a sports hall, village or community hall would be best as they do not tend to have carpeted floors. If you are having a summer wedding, you may like to hold the reception outside – even on the beach (although this may be somewhat risky given the British weather!). A marquee is another good option as it gives you a blank canvas to start with.

Clothing
So that everyone gets into the swing of the party, provide them with grass skirts and flower garlands (*lei*) as they enter the reception area. These may be worn over normal clothing for those who do not feel confident (or warm) enough to bare all.

Food
As guests enter the reception area, a beachcomber providing the costumes can welcome them. They may then be directed to a bar 'shack' where a variety of pretty cocktails should be served.

A barbecue with a buffet table of salads would be the obvious choice for this theme. Everyone should feel free to eat as and when they like throughout the reception. A selection of fresh fruits that may be picked at as people walk past would be a good option for dessert.

Alternatively, you might wish to stick with the cocktail party formula, and simply have canapés served by people dressed in Caribbean and Polynesian costume.

Decoration
With the tropical island theme, a good backdrop is essential if you are going to hold the party indoors. This can be made simply by painting a beach scene on sheeting hung from the walls, or could be hired from a theatrical company. Palm trees can be hired from a garden centre or plant hire specialist. Bamboo fencing may be used to surround the remainder of the room, and to create a bar 'shack'. To continue with this theme, lobster pots, coconuts, pineapples, a hammock, beach umbrellas, a canoe and a selection of boulders could be strategically placed around the room.

If you wish to create an 'evening in the tropics', lanterns could be used instead of the electric lights in the room. If this is not possible, you might like to consider hiring a 'star cloth' from a marquee company; this is a black cloth with several small holes which allow light through creating the effect of the night sky.

There are also specialist companies that hire props out for themed events such as this.

Music and entertainment

A steel band would provide the perfect entertainment for a Caribbean party. For anyone who may feel a little more energetic, you could arrange a limbo-dancing competition. Or why not hire a surfing simulator?

Alternatively, you may wish to arrange for a limbo-dancing display, and a group of Polynesian dancers to entertain your guests.

If you wish to continue into the evening with dancing, you might wish to engage a Beach Boys style band, or a disco in order that everyone's tastes are catered for.

Scottish baronial castle

Elements of this theme can be adopted from a medieval wedding theme, but taken further to embrace more of what Scotland has to offer.

Venue

A baronial hall or castle would be an ideal venue and some of these are licensed in the United Kingdom to hold wedding ceremonies. However, it is not difficult to create your own in any hotel banqueting suite. Again, either hiring equipment or making use of the services of your local amateur dramatics or theatre prop producers may be necessary.

Clothing

If the groom has great knees, this is the theme for him! Kilts are obligatory – what he wears underneath is up to him!

For the bride, quite an elaborate gown would be appropriate here. To maintain the Scottish theme, introducing some tartan, such as a sash, would be a nice touch.

Food

Instead of greeting guests to the reception with the obligatory sherry, buck's fizz or champagne, what about a whisky cocktail?

Don't like haggis? Have you tried it? Haggis, neeps and tatties would be the obvious choice for a Scottish meal ('neeps' being mashed turnips); however, a hearty beef or venison casserole would be a good alternative. Follow this with a flummery (syllabub containing whisky) and shortbread – what more do you need!

Decoration

A simple portcullis could be made to create a dramatic entrance through which guests enter the reception room. A backdrop of a baronial hall, complete with wooden panels, suits of armour, shields and swords hung on the wall could be set up. Swags of tartan can be hung to cover any curtains (lengths of fabric can be obtained from upholstery/fabric warehouses). Flags could be hung from the ceiling, if it is high enough, or around the walls. As this theme involves a formal, sit-down meal, the tables should be set for a banquet, complete with wrought-iron candle sticks. Ivy trailing from the candlesticks will soften the effect.

Music and entertainment

After the ceremony, if you have sufficient ushers dressed in highland attire, arrange to leave the church under an arch of swords. These can, again, be obtained from your local theatre group or props department.

On your arrival at the reception, or after the civil ceremony, guests could be greeted by a piper.

If you have access to gardens at your reception, you may wish to arrange for a little grouse shooting (clay or laser!). Guests may also be entertained after the meal by watching a little sword dancing while they allow their food to settle.

After this, a ceilidh band can be employed for the rest of the evening, or, alternatively, a disco.

Other cultural themes

The choice of cultural themes is wide, and here is a list of options:

- Austrian Tyrollean
- English boating theme
- English country wedding
- Barn dance
- Mardi Gras

- Arabian Souk
- Spanish Flamenco

Seasonal themes

If you are particularly attracted to one festive occasion throughout the year, why not marry at that time and theme your wedding to take advantage of the season. Flowers of the season will not be difficult to find, nor expensive to buy; other symbols of major holidays are widely recognized so co-ordinating all the aspects of your wedding should not be a problem. Most props should be easily obtainable from major department stores, or if you wish to take your ideas further, a specific party shop. In this section we look at various seasonal themes, presented according to their position in the annual calendar.

Christmas/New Year/winter

Often the period between Christmas and New Year is a very quiet one for the wedding industry, and many of your proposed guests will be on holiday from work. What better time to get married with everyone available! You may even be able to negotiate some discounts simply because this is a quiet time of year.

If you want to get married later in the day remember that you will only be able to have indoor photographs. Realistically, a wedding after 2 p.m. is unlikely to provide the photographer with enough light to take photographs both at the ceremony venue and outside at the reception venue.

Clothing

A wealth of party clothes will have been available in the shops since September! If you are to hold your ceremony in a hotel or other licensed venue, why not dress to kill, and have a late afternoon ceremony, with a black tie dinner: the ultimate sophistication.

If you wish to have a traditional church wedding, remember that it will be cold! The bride should consider wearing a fur-trimmed, hooded cloak, matched with a long-sleeved dress. She may wish to carry a fur-edged or lined muff to keep her hands warm, rather than carrying a bouquet. Consider also the colour of the dress; if it does snow, the whole effect of wearing a white dress may be lost. It may be better to consider an 'old gold', or 'café au lait' dress to contrast with the cold of winter, bringing a little warmth into the photographs.

Choose a warm colour for bridesmaids; blues and pale mauve appear cold, whereas apricot, red and burgundy colours give a warm feeling. Such colours would also allow the bride to choose white, green and gold floral arrangements which are more readily available at this time of year than the yellows and pinks of spring and summer.

Venue and decoration
During the winter months, you might feel that a reception held indoors is the best option. However, enquire of marquee companies; it is possible that you could arrange an extremely reasonable deal at this time of the year as they are often not busy now, and marquees are entirely capable of being heated. December and early January are also not always as cold as you might think.

Hotels, too, may offer good deals as they are about to pass into one of their quietest times of the year. If you are to marry between Christmas and New Year, you will find that most hotels are festively decorated and you may not need anything further. However, once into the New Year, everything will be looking a little tired, and you will probably wish to bring in some bright, colourful decorations to counteract the bleak weather outside!

Most flowers are very expensive at this time of year; use alternatives such as balloons, dried flowers, or a range of candles that will create a romantic feel in the dark of the mid to late afternoon. Alternatively, you may like to create a 'winter wonderland'; if you are to have a disco or band, create a 'wooded clearing' around the stage with pine trees (Christmas trees in pots obtained from any garden centre). Cover them with artificial snow and cobwebs. You may be able to obtain some 'winter' props from a local theatrical group, such as mountain scenery, etc., or make them yourself painted onto lengths of sheeting. Tables could be adorned with lanterns containing candles instead of flowers, with ivy spread over the tables.

Christmas decorations are good for creating a 'snowy' atmosphere – look out for silver and white decorations such as large foil or paper 'snowdrops' that may be hung from the ceiling, spray snow and cobwebs, etc.

If you wish to bring in a little fun, contact your local charity organizations, such as the Lions Club, who very often collect for charity before the Christmas period with reindeer and sleigh. For a donation, you are sure to be able to secure that float for an eye-catching display!

Another option is to follow a Scottish/tartan theme. Walls and windows could be decorated with swags of tartan, and bows tied to the backs of chairs.

Food
Guests will undoubtedly be cold when they arrive! Offer some good, spiced mulled wine or mulled ale when greeting them as an alternative to the traditional sherry or buck's fizz.

At this time of year, everyone has had their fill of roast meals, fancy food and nibbles; why not offer something much more plain and warming such as bangers and mash, or fish and chips, followed by a traditional English steamed pudding.

If you are choosing a tartan theme, go with the traditional Scottish foods – if you don't fancy the idea of haggis, why not choose a rich beef or venison casserole. This could be followed by a flummery and shortbread.

Music and entertainment
A winter wonderland wedding allows any form of entertainment; from a disco, to a string quartet to a full dance band. However, if you wish for music to be played during the meal, taped seasonal music is available in most good music stores.

For a tartan New Year's wedding, a piper is a must! A piper can announce your arrival to and exit from the ceremony, and play at the entrance to your reception to entertain your guests as they line up to congratulate you.

After the meal, a Scottish ceilidh band would keep everyone on their toes, children and grannies alike!

Summer/seashore

If you live near the sea, a beach party would provide an unusual, but entirely acceptable wedding reception.

If this is not possible, the summer sun/beach atmosphere can be re-created in any available venue, but would be best in a marquee, hall or garden.

Clothing
It is unlikely that you would want to wear a swimsuit for a wedding, but it's your wedding, so do what you wish! You

might even choose to dress as a mermaid or merman! Possibly a more acceptable style of dress for the bride would be short, with lace shells attached. A summery dress and strappy flat sandals would be entirely appropriate, with flowers pinned into her hair, a headdress made of shells, or a large floppy sun hat.

The men in the wedding party might choose to wear shorts, loud shirts and beach caps – whatever you feel comfortable in would be appropriate. Guests should be warned – this could be the opportunity to wear that awful shirt they picked up in Hawaii and have never dared to wear again!

Venue and decoration
If you are marrying in licensed premises, arrange for the standard seating to be removed, and deck chairs installed. Beach towels could be placed for you to stand on during the ceremony, and the room decorated with large shells, lobster baskets and fishing nets.

The reception venue can, again, be furnished with beach chairs, lobster baskets, coils of rope, fishing nets and a small boat. Baskets of shells, or one large shell can be used as a table decoration, together with storm lanterns containing a lighted candle.

Again, you might be able to produce a seaside backdrop by painting on sheeting hung from the walls, or speak with your local theatrical company for any assistance or props that they may have.

Food
If you and your guests like it, seafood would be a good option. With the variety that is available, a buffet with prawns, salmon, and other fish dishes accompanied by salads would ensure that everyone got something that they liked.

Another appropriate meal would be a 'beach barbecue', again served with salads on a buffet. This type of food may be eaten either standing or sitting, according to the location of your reception.

Music and entertainment
If you choose a reception on the beach, the main form of entertainment needs to be mobile, relying on little or no power. Discos generally run from mains electricity, but it may be worth trying to find one that has a generator and is capable of running anywhere. However, this may prove unpopular with other people living in the vicinity, and you would need to ask

permission of the local council. A better option would be for you to provide music by means of a battery-powered, portable CD/cassette player.

If you have an indoor venue, to remain in keeping with the theme, a Beach Boys style band would provide suitable music, which is easy for everyone to dance to.

Other seasonal themes

Here are some further ideas for seasonal themes:

- St Valentine's Day
- Easter/spring
- May Day
- 4th of July
- Harvest/autumn
- November 5 (Bonfire night)
- Halloween.

Fantasy themes

For something unique, fun and totally individual, you might wish to choose a theme for its theatrical qualities. There is nothing real about the following themes – they are just pure fantasy. Depending on the theme chosen, these may be a little more difficult than other themes for your guests to join in with. However, given sufficient notice, most people will make the effort.

Ideally, guests should come dressed the part; if this is not appropriate, provide them with props, such as hats, ties or other accessories. These are normally available either by mail order, or from good party shops or department stores. It is worth looking out for goodies that are available at different times of the year celebrating recognized festivals which may be appropriate to your chosen fantasy theme.

Hollywood

Imagine the 'Oscars'; this is what you are trying to re-create. The timing of your wedding is important, as to hold an evening like this the ceremony must be as late in the day as possible. If you choose a 5 p.m. wedding, this would fit in nicely as, after time has been taken up with photographs and pre-dinner drinks, the meal can be served at 7 p.m.

Everything should be bright, shining and glamorous.

Venue

This theme is ideally suited to a smart hotel, with a large banqueting hall and stage. The overall scheme is very glitzy and glamorous, and the hotel should provide a dramatic backdrop for your ceremony.

They should be able to provide a silver service banquet, with champagne/sparkling wine in silver ice-buckets beside each table. All the tables should be immaculate, with polished silver and glass adorning the table.

Clothing

Evening dress is the order of the day, with men in black tie, and ladies in long evening dresses.

This is not the occasion to dress down! It is your opportunity to wear the most glamourous clothes you have ever seen in your life – and to get away with it without looking completely over the top!

The bride should consider having her dress specially made to suit the occasion, or should look around the shops in October and November, just before the party season commences. There will undoubtedly be a whole host of gowns that would be appropriate. If the groom does not have a dinner suit, these may be easily hired from any good menswear hire company.

Transport

Go for glamour – hire a stretch limousine! These are available mainly in either white or black, but are a little more expensive to hire than the more standard Rolls Royce, Mercedes or Volvo. At least you should only have to hire one – everyone will fit in the same car!

Food

The food served at your banquet must be excellent, and impressive. Serve canapés with drinks before the main banquet, and, if you can afford it, serve more, smaller courses than the standard three. The greatest attention to detail must be given to presentation. Although the overall quantity need not be greater than normal, the overall effect should be one of opulence.

Decoration

Lowered lighting, with candelabras on the tables, sets the scene. Large, fresh floral arrangements can be used to decorate the edge of the stage area and around the room. Table-centre decorations should either surround a candelabra or contain candles to light the room. Glitter stars sprinkled on the tables under the table settings would catch the flickering candles, giving a sparkled effect to the room.

Glitter curtains can be used to cover doorways, and to decorate either side of the stage and as a backdrop to it. Spotlighting the musicians playing on the stage would also add a glamourous feel.

Music and entertainment

Having a toastmaster in full uniform to announce guests as they arrive makes guests feel welcomed and important. After the welcoming drinks, another nice touch would be for waiters to lead guests to their allocated table and assist them in getting seated for the meal.

After the meal, a cabaret band with singers would add the necessary glamour to the occasion. They are generally very versatile, and able to sing music from a variety of eras. You might also like to engage a group of dancers, a magician or other cabaret act.

Carnival

Create a carnival atmosphere with a Mardi Gras theme. This is another theme that is easy for guests to feel a part of; providing them with a simple Mardi Gras mask enables them to join in and let their hair down.

Venue

If you are able to marry at a venue very local to your own home, consider having a procession/street party from your door to the ceremony venue. This could be led by various members of your family, followed by the bridesmaids and finally by the bride and her father. After the ceremony, the procession could be led by the bride and groom to their reception venue.

Any hall or hotel would be suitable for a Mardi Gras party, or even a street party if you live in a suitable location but you'll need consent from the police and local authority first.

Clothing

Mardi Gras is a huge party; wear what you like as long as it is colourful and easy to move in. For inspiration, look at the Notting Hill carnival – colourful jesters, musicians, jugglers, show girls and stilt walkers.

Bright coloured, sparkly party-wear is a good choice, although you do need to create a relaxed atmosphere.

Transport

As mentioned above, a procession to the wedding from your home would be a fun way to commence the day. However, this may not be practical, and so another form of transport might have to be chosen. A horse and carriage may be decorated with balloons and streamers, with feathers adorning the horse, and this could all become part of the themed celebration.

Food

If you are able to hold a street party, a barbecue or cold finger buffet would be the best option for feeding your guests.

If you are transforming a hotel room or hall, the choice with regard to food is up to you, it could be either a stand-up buffet or a sit-down meal.

Decoration

Whatever decorations you choose, they must be bright. Balloons, streamers and bunting are the cheapest way of decorating a large area. Musical props can be hired from theatrical companies, or plastic imitations are available for decoration purposes. Comedy/ tragedy masks are the traditional face of Mardi Gras and should appear somewhere within the overall theme, either as table centres or as wall decorations.

Masks, whistles, streamers, blowers and flags for waving should all be provided for guests to get into the party mood.

Music and entertainment

Mardi Gras is all about colour, action and music. A jazz band is ideal for this theme – you may like to consider a walk-about jazz band playing whilst you are welcoming your guests and whilst welcome drinks and dinner are served. A full jazz band with singer could then take over later in the evening, with a disco to follow for dancing later in the evening.

In addition to this, you might wish to consider hiring a magician, stilt walkers or jugglers and jesters to keep your guests entertained.

Other fantasy themes

The only limit to the range of fantasy themes is your imagination. Further ideas include:

- circus
- fairground
- horror

- school days
- pirate
- wild west.

Design your own theme

Every couple will have some limitations to consider. The amount you are able to spend is one of the most important considerations, as it would be unwise to commence married life with a great deal of debt. (We look at weddings on a budget in Chapter 9.) Perhaps you have a favourite restaurant and would like to hold your reception there; it may be insufficiently large to accommodate the number of guests that you wish to invite. Daydreams of the perfect wedding often have to be compromised upon, but it is best to do this earlier rather than later.

If you are considering an alternative celebration, think about the guests that you wish to attend. If you have a large number of elderly relatives to be invited to the wedding, consider the building in which you are to marry – for example, is the access adequate? A wedding that is too unusual may also make them feel uncomfortable, and unless forewarned, they will be unprepared for the festivities you have planned. You might wish to consider enclosing a note with the invitation if you are planning something very different from the norm.

The number of guests to be invited may also affect the style of wedding you decide upon. For example, if you have a large budget, there would be no problem with hiring a marquee and undertaking an exotic theme with several entertainers. If your budget is limited, you will need to be inventive if you wish to ask a large number of guests. It is better to invite fewer guests and let them enjoy a high-quality reception, than to have more guests and try to stretch your budget by finding the cheapest possible suppliers. Cheaper quotations may well omit hidden extras.

In earlier chapters, many popular and unusual themes have been covered; however, you might want something more suited to your own backgrounds, careers, personalities or personal interests.

To give you the general idea, let's look at one multi-cultural couple who married recently:

Bride:	English	Groom:	Sri Lankan
	Doctor		Doctor
	Interested in travel		Loves jazz music

This couple's official wedding ceremony was a very traditional English ceremony, in a country church. The bride wore a white wedding dress.

After the wedding they went to the bride's home where a marquee had been erected in the garden. Within the marquee a *chuppah* had been erected (a canopy covered with flowers). The bride then changed into a sari, and a Hindu ceremony was performed under the *chuppah*. After the ceremony, guests were treated to a traditional English wedding breakfast.

After the couple returned from their honeymoon, a second reception party was held in an old country barn. Guests mainly wore Sri Lankan dress, and the food served was Sri Lankan curries. Again, the bride wore a sari. The music playing was, of course, a jazz band.

As you can see, this wedding encompassed both traditions of English and Sri Lankan ceremonies, together with the interests of the couple.

To develop a theme entirely suited to you, take an evening out to brainstorm the possibilities. Write down on a sheet of paper everything about yourselves, your interests, your backgrounds and your hopes for the future. Write down everything, from the silliest of things to the more mundane. Not only will this give you a basis from which to work, but you may learn more about each other in the process!

For inspiration, look at society, wedding and fashion magazines; look at features on society functions; books on the history of fashion, decorative design and art can also be helpful; use the library! If you still feel that you are missing the mark, consider using a professional consultant or party planner who will be able to assist with drawing your ideas together into an overall theme.

Keep bouncing around the ideas for a few days or weeks, if you have time. When you feel that you have exhausted the subject, go back through your lists and discard those that you feel are irrelevant. Keep going through the lists until you have got down to the best ideas, draw them all together and think about ways to implement them. Think about ways in which you can personalize all areas of the celebration, such as the following:

- the form of the ceremony – music, hymns, readings, vows and blessings
- the location of the ceremony and reception
- invitations, reply cards, menus, order of service, etc.
- catering and beverages – consider period, ethnic and regional foods
- the cake – get away from the traditional and consider a specially designed masterpiece
- the colour scheme for decorations and bridal wear
- the style of bridal wear – do you really want to stick with the traditional white gown?
- costumes for guests, or serving/waiting staff and hired performers
- flowers, decorations, and symbols
- transport – consider unique conveyances, such as a bus, the Batmobile, or Trotter's Independent Traders three-wheeler!
- photography – colour, black and white or DIY?
- gifts – do you really need a gift list if you are already living together? Consider asking for money for either a fabulous honeymoon, or to use as an investment
- music and entertainment – including musicians, magicians, sketch artists, etc.

Designing your own theme is a challenge – but it is also enormous fun!

Occupational themes

Using your career as a basis for a theme is an excellent idea. It can be formal or informal, serious or light but is one of the easier ways to theme your wedding as, generally speaking, symbols of your profession are easily recognized. The following are some examples for different professions. Remember to be sensitive to hidden pitfalls. For example, 'impersonating' a police officer or member of the armed services isn't considered amusing by many involved in those professions, or by older members of the community who might have been involved in conflict or emergencies. In the wrong place at the wrong time it could even be an offence in law.

Musicians
You could use musical instruments as décor and as a cake design. The comedy/tragedy masks of drama could be used on stationery, and large cut-outs of them used to decorate the room.

Doctors
Dressed in white coats, doctors could arrive at the ceremony in an ambulance, and have 'black bag' party boxes given to guests with their canapés or buffet inside.

Lawyers

Both barristers and solicitors may wear wigs and robes and carry gavels, with a 'law book' cake. Guests may like to take part in a 'murder mystery' as entertainment for the evening!

Teachers

You could have mathematical problems on invitations, wear mortar boards and robes at the reception, use a blackboard for the menu and have a cake in the shape of a school building.

Estate agents

The venue for your reception can be decorated with 'sale boards' wishing good luck, mobile phones and property particulars could be dotted around the room, and you could arrive in a flashy car and have a country-cottage styled cake.

Office staff and computer operators

Invitations, menus and order of service sheets could be typed on continuous stationery, and the cake could be in the form of a typewriter or computer.

Members of the police force

Dressed in uniform, you could arrive at the ceremony in a police car. You could also have napkin rings shaped like handcuffs, a cake that is in the form of a jail, blue flashing lights as table centres and invitations in the form of a summons.

Members of the armed forces

Again, you could be dressed in uniform, have a cake in the form of a tank, ship or submarine – and even arrive at the ceremony in an armoured vehicle! Patriotic flags and banners could be used to decorate the room.

Graphic designers and architects

Employ your artistic talents and design beautiful stationery. Elements of the design can also be recreated in floral arrangements or balloon decorations. An unusual 'building' could be used as the basis for your cake, or, alternatively, tools of the trade might provide you with some inspiration.

Gardeners

This theme is suitable for anyone working with plants, or who gardens as a hobby, and you can choose to use a variety of plants and flowers throughout the celebration. Think also about using gardening implements and accessories, such as plant labels for place names, wheelbarrows and buckets for holding floral arrangements, and having a 'potting shed' cake.

Farmers

An ideal venue might be a barn, which you could decorate using sacks, bales and wheat sheaves alongside the foliage and flowers that are abundant in the countryside. Stationery in the shape of or showing animals, corn ears or tractors would be appropriate, and may also be used for the design of your cake. Corn ears placed in the folds of napkins on tables look very effective.

As you can imagine, it would be impossible to cover every profession in this section, but hopefully these ideas will give you some inspiration.

Locational themes

Another way to theme your wedding to suit you is to think of a place that is special to you. For example, if the groom proposed whilst on holiday abroad with the bride, recreate that country and their customs for your wedding.

Alternatively, a bride may like to return to the place where the groom popped the question, for the celebration. This may mean a marriage abroad.

Heritage themes

Another way of embracing your different backgrounds is by looking to your heritage for inspiration. Ask relatives about the location, profession and interests of your ancestors; you may find that you have relatives with a colourful background, such as a music hall singer, a gypsy, a baron or a lord. These could all be developed into a theme for your wedding.

If either you or your ancestors originated from different countries, bring these together in a joint ceremony. There are several ways suggested in this book for bringing together different aspects of different cultures with symbols and ceremonies. If you feel that having a double ceremony, or trying to encompass rituals from different cultures is too difficult, consider just using the flags of the different nations as a base for your theme. For example, if an English person is to marry a American, use the combined flags of the different nations on your stationery. Use flags and banners to decorate your venue; sprinkle glitter stars on the tables that have been covered with starred cloths; have small flags as table centres – you get the idea!

If there are to be guests from different cultures at your wedding breakfast, consider having two buffet areas. For example, if an

English person is to marry an Indian person, consider having one buffet area serving Indian food, and one buffet area serving English food. This would keep even the most uncompromising guest happy!

Special interest/hobby weddings

One of the most common ways that couples meet is through a shared hobby. Consider using this hobby as a basis for your theme. Theming ideas for some hobbies are given below; again, symbols from your chosen hobby are generally recognizable and easy for guests to embrace.

Diving

Although such a marriage might not be legal in the United Kingdom, there are some countries in the world where ceremonies underwater are performed. This might involve a separate ceremony with a local registrar or minister of justice to ensure its legality. It would be difficult to organize an underwater wedding yourself, and you should therefore refer to a specialist travel operator who will be able to assist you.

Sailing

Marriages performed at sea are not legal in the United Kingdom. However, some ships' captains are licensed to perform marriage ceremonies aboard foreign registered vessels.

If you wish to marry on board a vessel, there are permanently moored boats that are licensed for the performance of wedding ceremonies. For example, the T S *Queen Mary*, which is moored on Victoria Embankment in London, is licensed and can provide your wedding breakfast and evening reception on board as well.

If travelling to London for your ceremony on water is not possible, several vessels are available for hire throughout the country that offer on-site catering facilities. However, they may not be able to accommodate a large party, and you might have to restrict the number of guests you invite.

Skiing

Several companies now offer skiing holiday weddings as well as the more common tropical beach ceremony. Again, contact a specialist wedding tour operator if you wish to marry abroad. Alternatively, adopt some of the symbols of skiing into your ceremony, such as using skis as decorations, etc. You might like to adopt some of the elements from the winter theme mentioned earlier.

Flying

Once again, a legal ceremony in the air is not possible in the United Kingdom. However, you could choose a 'Biggles' or 'Magnificent Men in their Flying Machines' type theme, with guests wearing flying helmets and scarves; a bi-plane cake; miniature aircraft hanging from the ceiling as decorations; lights 'runway' style running up the aisle; and flying 'log books' as invitations and menus.

Horse riding/show jumping

If you live close to an equestrian centre, you can approach them to see whether they would consider hiring out their venue for your reception. Unless this is in the middle of summer, however, it is likely to be quite a chilly venue.

Most racecourses have banqueting facilities, or you may consider hiring a box for your guests overlooking the course. Sandown Park racecourse is actually licensed to hold wedding ceremonies!

Another option would be to recreate an indoor show arena, with flags and jumps. Seat people around the edge of the room and have a band playing in the centre of the ring. If you wish to entertain your guests in a slightly different way, why not engage an event organizer and arrange a race night!

Camping

This theme would seem to suggest a marquee. However, extend your thinking a little further and consider a 'scouting/guiding' theme, with tents surrounding a central area, which may be used for a barbecue or buffet. You might wish to consider a 'sausage sizzle' over an open fire, and finish up with a good old sing-song.

Racing

Many racetracks today offer corporate entertainment facilities. If you are a racing enthusiast, it is worth approaching your local racetrack to enquire about your wedding reception. Guests may also like the opportunity of having a quick spin around the track! If you wish to create the racing atmosphere at another venue, use chequered flags, bunting and champagne bottles to decorate the room; trophies can be used as table decorations, and you must arrive in a classic racing car.

Karting venues also offer corporate hospitality days; if karting is more to your taste, approach your local track to see whether they would be able to help you.

Tennis

Using the symbols and colours of Wimbledon, recreate your own sporting occasion. Racquets can be depicted on stationery; tennis balls used within decorations, trophies used as table centres, and the colours must, of course, be green and purple. And what else, other than strawberries and cream for dessert!

Gambling

If you like a little flutter, why not organize a casino for your guests. Great fun, and no-one loses any money! This could be combined with a Prohibition, 1920s, or Las Vegas style theme – unusual for a wedding, but it's your chance to do what you want!

Bowling

There are several ten-pin bowling alleys around the country now that offer hospitality packages. If you would like an active wedding reception, hire the whole venue and arrange for guests to play as and when they like. Catering is usually fairly basic and would suit a wide variety of tastes. You would not have to worry about entertaining any children at the reception – they would be far too busy enjoying themselves!

Miscellaneous

If you are just looking for an unusual venue in which to hold your ceremony or reception, nowadays you will be spoilt for choice. The number of licensed venues is increasing all the time, and today includes such unusual places as London Zoo, Bentley Wildfowl and Motor Museum, Sandown Park Racecourse, 007 Bond Street (James Bond memorabilia club), and the Pinewood Studies. Many golf clubs, castles, hotels and stately homes also have licences.

If you have a venue in mind, there is no harm in approaching them to see whether they would be prepared to hire you the venue. Facilities such as marquees, caterers, toilets and everything you need to make your day perfect are available from a variety of suppliers, or you can hire a wedding co-ordinator to assist you.

Whatever your interests, whatever your dream, with a little thought and planning, you can make it happen!

08
wedding planner

This chapter contains models for a number of lists and reminders that you might find helpful when trying to keep track of all the things that need to be done in the next few weeks and months.

The 'Countdown – nine months to wedding day' (see page 170) shows an example of a wedding planned with nine months in which to do it all. The format can be adapted easily to suit any period and to reflect your own priorities.

The 'Budget form' (see page 173) is to remind you of the items you will, or may wish, to buy. All the standard items are listed, to help make sure nothing important is overlooked, and there are two spare spaces, marked as 'Other' at the bottom in case you want to add anything else. The 'Contingency' space is for an additional percentage to take care of the unexpected or suddenly-more-expensive-than-you-first-thought additions to the budget. If you're pretty good at working out planning budgets, you may need to add only around 5 per cent to the total but, if you're uncertain when it comes to looking ahead, nearer 10 per cent would be wise. The Budget form is the first shot, the means by which you can determine how much, or little, you want to spend on each item before you begin to look around for suppliers and ask for estimates. Both the Budget form and the Suppliers and costs form will help you keep track of how close your original plan was to reality and allow you to revise your forecasts as you go along.

Next come the more specific issues, especially related to collecting information from traders and suppliers of wedding services. In requesting information it is quite important to ask each different trader for exactly the same thing. That sounds like a statement of the obvious but it is very easy to fall into agreement with someone who is trying to be helpful, by suggesting little additions and refinements that sound interesting, then find that you have collected three different quotations for three rather different things instead of the same one. The 'Quotation/Estimate specification' record (see page 174) is designed to help you avoid that problem.

The 'Suppliers and costs' record keeps track of which people you've spoken too, when you contacted them and what prices they quoted. Bear in mind that price does not always reflect quality and it is a good idea to ask for a sample, or to see an example, to satisfy yourself before making a commitment.

On page 179 you will find an example of how you might fill in the Suppliers and Costs record. You might like to record details directly in this book, or you might prefer to copy the example into your wedding file or folder. Keeping track of the timetable and your expenditure will help you to stay calm and relaxed, knowing that everything is under control and in hand.

Most of the quotes/estimates you collect will be actual costs; for example, when the transport company say that the bridal limousine you want to hire will cost £390, that will almost always be the actual price you will pay, even if the wedding is 12 months away. It is always a good idea to ask, and confirm the position just in case but, as a rule, that is the way the wedding market works.

It can, however, be a little misleading at times. Prices sometimes seem rather high until you remember that the quote you receive today is for a service you will receive several months in the future and, by accepting the quotation, you should be guaranteeing that there will be no price increase in the meantime. That is the main reason why it is good practice to check the basis of the supplier's quote before agreeing to it.

These models of reminders and lists are just a few of many you, and others involved in planning, could use. They are all flexible and easily adapted to suit the best man, the bride's mother and so on, according to need.

Countdown – nine months to wedding day (WD)

Week	To do	By whom?	Done (✓)
37	Tell parents and arrange for them to meet if they do not already know each other	B & G	
36	Make a list of everyone to tell	B, G, PB, PG	
35	Notify family and friends	B, G, PB, PG	
	Arrange press announcements	BP	
34	Decide on style and type of wedding	B, G, BP	
	Begin research on reception venues	MB, B, G	
33	Continue research on reception venues	MB, B, G	

Week	To do	By whom?	Done (✓)
33	Make appointment to visit minister/priest, if appropriate	B, G	
32	Visit a short list of reception venues	MB, B, G	
31/30	Book reception venue and church for wedding date	MB, B, G	
29	Begin compiling guest list	B, G, PB, PG	
28	Begin research on all other suppliers	MB, B, G, BM, CB	
27	Finalize Order of Service with minister/priest	MB, B, G	
26	Draft a rough budget of available finance	B, G, PB, PG	
25			
24	Decide on bridesmaids and ask them	B	
	Begin looking at wedding gown/outfit designs	MB, B	
	Choose and order stationery	MB, B, G	
23	Book honeymoon and apply for passports	G (& B)	
22	Begin choosing and booking other suppliers. Continue until all services confirmed	MB, B, G, BM, CB	
21	Choose best man and ask him	G	
	Choose wedding gown/outfit, plan shopping/dressmaker visit and so on	MB, B, CB	
20/19	Choose and book traders/suppliers	B, PB	
18	Update draft budget based on quotes	B, PB	
17			
16	Choose church music	B, G	
15			
14	Choose and order bridesmaids' dresses	B, CB, MB	
13	Choose and order/book last traders/suppliers	B, MB, G	
	Draw up gift list	B, MB, G	
12	Send out invitations and gift list	MB, B	
11	Visit registrar, if appropriate	B, G	
10	Choose and book florist*	B, MB	

Week	To do	By whom?	Done (✓)
9	Book hairdresser and beauty therapist, if home visit on wedding day is required*	B, CB	
	Choose and reserve men's outfits*	G, U, BM, FB, FG	
8	Arrange rehearsal	B, G	
7	Arrange wedding night accommodation	G	
6	Buy gifts for attendants	B, G	
	Brief attendants on duties	B, G	
5	Buy rings	B, G	
	Medical/health for honeymoon	B, G	
	Arrange Stag/Hen nights	CB, BM	
4	Dress fittings (if made to measure)	B, CB, Br	
	Choose going-away outfits	G, BM, B, CB	
	Stag/Hen nights	BM, G, B, CB, Br	
3	Arrange press announcements	P, B	
	Check honeymoon tickets, etc.	G	
	Draft speeches	G, BM, FB	
2	Rehearsal (church only)	B, G, PB, PG, BM, CB, U, Br	
	Final dress fittings	B, Br, CB	
1	Check and confirm all traders/suppliers	MB, B	
	Delegate all wedding day tasks	B, G, PB	
1 day	Check all certificates and licences	B, G	
	Orders of service to best man (unless other arrangements made)	B	
	Dresses collected or delivered	B, Br, CB	
	Pack for wedding night/honeymoon	B, G	
	Check transport away from reception	G	
WD	Relax	All	

Key

MB	= Mother of the bride	B	= Bride
FB	= Father of the bride	G	= Groom
PB	= Parents of the bride	PG	= Parents of the groom
CB	= Chief bridesmaid	FG	= Father of the groom
U	= Ushers	Br	= Bridesmaids
BM	= Best man	M	= Minister
*	= Preferably done earlier – last chance!		

Budget form

Service	Estimate	Agreed cost	Actual cost
Bridal gown			
Bridal accessories			
Bridesmaids' dresses			
Bridesmaids' accessories			
Children's outfits			
Menswear			
Rings			
Cake			
Attendants' gifts			
Stationery and postage			
Photography			
Video			
Flowers			
Balloons			
Transport			
Entertainment			
Reception (catered but ex. wine)			
Wine (with the meal and for toast)			
Funding for the bar			
Honeymoon			
Other			
Other			
Contingency			
Total			

Quotation/Estimate specification

Examples

Specification – flowers

The bridal bouquet is to be made of cream gardenias and cream and red roses with ferns and ivy trailing in a pear-drop shape approximately 30 cm (12 inches) wide at its widest point and 60 cm (24 inches) at its longest.

Four bridesmaids will carry a circular posy each, approximately 15 cm (6 inches) in diameter, made of cream gardenias and deep pink carnations.

Five buttonholes: 2 x red roses and 3 x cream roses.

Photography

Twenty colour and fifteen black and white pictures to be displayed in a cream leather souvenir binder, style number 0000, (with pockets for other items).

Bridal veil

Ivory veil in fine net gathered into comb, with over face fall of 60 cm (24 inches) and back fall 2 m (6ft 6in) long (to match the train on the dress). Veil to be trimmed with Nottingham lace edging 10 cm (4 inches) wide (butterfly design).

Suppliers and costs

For the wedding of .... and ....

on .... (date)

Service	Supplier/ trader	Date contacted	Price quoted	Accepted	Actual cost	Paid (✓)
Reception venue						
Photographer						
Video						
Florist						
Transport						
Bridal gown						

Service	Supplier/ trader	Date contacted	Price quoted	Accepted	Actual cost	Paid (✓)
Bride's shoes						
Bride's veil						
Bride's headdress						
Bride's lingerie						
Bridesmaids' dresses						
Bridesmaids' shoes						
Bridesmaids' headdresses						

Service	Supplier/ trader	Date contacted	Price quoted	Accepted	Actual cost	Paid (✓)
Attendants' gifts						
Groom's outfit						
Bride's father's outfit						
Bride's mother's outfit						
Rings						
Balloons						
Stationery and postage						

Service	Supplier/ trader	Date contacted	Price quoted	Accepted	Actual cost	Paid (✓)
Cake						
Make-up						
Hairdresser						
Church/ register office fees						
Entertainment						
Other						

Example

Service	Supplier/ trader	Date contacted	Price quoted	Accepted	Actual cost	Paid (✓)
Reception venue	Raven Hotel	4 Aug	£62.50	No		
	Crescent Hotel	8 Aug	£64.75	No		
	Albany Hotel	11 Aug	£58.25	Yes	£58.25 per head	✓
Photographer	You've Been Framed	16 Sept	£850.00			
	Callan Photo.	18 Sept				
	Ivan's Camera Shop					

Wedding day timetables

The following tables model typical wedding day programmes, one for a church wedding and one for a register office wedding. You might like to adapt these to your own circumstances and use them as a diary-cum-reminder. By the time you reach the stage of actually working out what you will be doing on 'The Day' you will probably be feeling excited, nervous and wondering how you could ever have thought that you were different from everyone else in believing that arranging your wedding would be easy!

Many brides have gone down this path before you and have survived to enjoy and celebrate their wedding days so don't worry, you're nearly there and there's not long to wait now.

Church wedding

Ceremony due to begin at 2.30 p.m.

Where	What	When
Bride's home	The bride, her parents and attendants are preparing for the ceremony	10.30 a.m.
	Flowers arrive	
Best man's home	Best man is preparing for the ceremony	11.30 a.m.
Bride's home	Bride's mother rings reception venue to check everything OK	12.00 p.m.
	Best man arrives to collect buttonholes for himself, groom and ushers	12.15 p.m.
Groom's home	Groom and his parents are preparing for the ceremony	12.30 p.m.
Ushers' homes	Ushers are preparing for the ceremony	
Groom's home	Best man arrives	1.00 p.m.
Church	Ushers arrive and prepare prayer and hymn books/orders of service, check out seating and parking	1.45 p.m.
Groom's home	Best man calls bride's father to let him know he and groom are leaving for the church	1.45 p.m.
Bride's home	Limousine(s) arrives	1.50 p.m.
Church	Groom and best man arrive: buttonholes and orders of service given to ushers	2.00 p.m.
	Best man finds minister and pays church fees	
	Guests begin to arrive, ushers give them orders of service/books, escort to seats and warn guests of camera/confetti restrictions	2.10 p.m.
Bride's home	Bride's mother and attendants leave for the church	2.10 p.m.
	Bride and father leave for church	2.20 p.m.
	Bells begin, choir enters the church	2.20 p.m.

Where	What	When
Church	Bride's mother and attendants arrive	2.25 p.m.
	Bride and father arrive, groom and best man move into position, bride and father, with attendants, progress up aisle	2.30 p.m.
	Ceremony begins	
	Progress out of church, photo session outside	3.20 p.m.
	Bride and groom leave for reception	4.00 p.m.
	Parents, attendants and guests leave for reception	4.05 p.m.
Reception	Parents, best man and chief bridesmaid arrive, reception line forms	4.15 p.m.
	Newly-weds arrive	4.20 p.m.
	Guests arrive and are welcomed	4.25 p.m.
	Meal is served	5.00 p.m.
	Speeches	5.40 p.m.
	Cake cutting	6.00 p.m.
	Party/Dancing begins	6.10 p.m.
	Bride and groom leave	10.30 p.m.
	Guests and attendants begin to leave	10.45 p.m.
	Reception ends; best man and chief bridesmaid take care of any clothes left by the bride and groom, and repack wedding gifts for journey to newly-weds'/ parent's home, bride's parents check reception area for lost property, etc. and thank staff	11.00 p.m.
	Bride's parents, best man and chief bridesmaid leave	11.20 p.m.

Register office

Ceremony due to begin at 11.15 a.m.

Where	What	When
Bride's home	Bride, her parents and matron-of-honour are preparing for the ceremony	8.15 a.m.
	Flowers arrive	
Best man's home	Best man is preparing for the ceremony	9.30 a.m.
Bride's home	Bride's mother rings reception venue to check everything OK	9.45 a.m.
	Best man arrives to collect buttonholes for himself and groom	9.50 a.m.
Groom's home	Groom and his parents are preparing for the ceremony	
	Best man arrives	10.00 a.m.
Bride's home	Limousine(s) arrives	10.35 a.m.
Groom's home	Best man calls bride's father to let him know he and groom are leaving for the register office	10.45 a.m.
Bride's home	Bride's mother and attendant leave	10.55 a.m.
Register office	Groom and best man arrive	11.00 a.m.
	Bride's mother and bride's attendant arrive	
	Guests begin to arrive	
	Bride and father arrive	11.15 a.m.
	Groom, best man and guests ushered into marriage room by registrar's assistant	11.15 a.m.
	Bride enters marriage room, ceremony commences	
	After ceremony, photo session	11.30 a.m.
	Newly-weds leave for reception	11.50 a.m.
	Parents, attendants and guests leave for reception	11.55 a.m.
Reception	Parents, best man and matron-of-honour arrive, reception line forms	12.05 p.m.

Where	What	When
	Newly-weds arrive	12.10 p.m.
	Guests arrive and are welcomed	12.15 p.m.
	Meal is served	12.45 p.m.
	Speeches	1.30 p.m.
	Cake cutting	1.55 p.m.
	Party/Dancing begins	2.30 p.m.
	Finger buffet set out by caterer	7.00 p.m.
	Bride and groom leave	9.30 p.m.
	Guests and attendants begin to leave	10.30 p.m.
	Reception ends; best man and matron-of-honour take care of any clothes left by the bride and groom, and repack wedding gifts for journey to newly-weds'/parent's home; bride's parents check reception area for lost property, etc. and thank staff	10.50 p.m.
	Last person leaves	11.00 p.m.

09

weddings on a budget

One thing that all couples are likely to have some concern about when planning their wedding is the cost – or at least, if they do not, their parents will!

Wedding magazines regularly review the cost of weddings; the average cost of getting married in 2004 was in the region of £16,000! Where does this all go? If you plan on a wedding based around the traditional style, with 120 guests, you can expect your money to be spent in the following ways.

Item	Budget
Engagement ring	850
Stationery	300
Bride's dress	1,000
Groom's outfit	500
Attendants' outfits	1,000
Church fees	500
Bride's wedding ring	210
Groom's wedding ring	175
Flowers	350
Photography	750
Video	750
Transport	350
Gifts for attendants and family	400
Hire of reception venue	750
Catering and food	3,000
Drink	700
Cake	250
Band	650
Bride's going-away outfit	350
First-night hotel	150
Honeymoon	3,000
Total	£15,985

Many couples are not able to spend such a large amount of money, and it is unwise to borrow and start married life in debt. So, if you have a budget – stick to it! Look at the items mentioned above, and decide what is important to you, and what is not. Open a separate savings account specifically for wedding expenses. Putting a little money aside each month is easier than finding a large sum just before the wedding day, particularly if you are also intending to buy a house (for which other expenses will crop up).

The engagement ring and party

It is unlikely that you will wish to try cutting costs on an engagement ring. This will last a lifetime, and is generally purchased sometime before the actual wedding. However, bear in mind that once engaged, you must now start to save for The Big Day – you may feel that you would like to spend a little less on the engagement ring, and start putting some money aside in a separate account for the wedding itself.

If you wish to have a party to celebrate your engagement, hold it at home and ask everyone to bring a bottle. If you do not have a large-enough house or garden, hire your local community hall and employ an outside bar service – they usually provide their services free of charge as they will make their money from the drinks sold. You do not have to provide food at such a gathering – just nibbles placed strategically around the room.

Invitations can be prepared on your computer, or a pad of invitations to be handwritten purchased from a good stationer. Balloons and streamers make good, cheap decorations.

Wedding stationery

The choice of wedding stationery on the market is enormous. It ranges from packs that are to be handwritten available from most good stationers, to a vast range of invitations, reply cards, menus, place name cards, order of service cards, napkins, book matches, coasters and cake boxes that can all be printed to your requirements. If you are trying to cut costs, most of this is an unnecessary expense that will not be noticed by your guests.

The cheapest stationery available can often be found advertised in wedding magazines, as supplements, and is available by mail order. You can also take advantage of special offers from stationery suppliers if you visit them whilst they are exhibiting at a local wedding fayre.

Invitations

If you do not wish to buy pre-packs of invitations to write yourself, why not make your own? Remember, cards do not have to be folded – a flat sheet of card or good quality paper is just as acceptable.

Computer-prepared invitations

If you have access to a computer, you will undoubtedly have access to a presentation package. There is a vast selection of clip-art available on most packages, and using this, combined with other freely available clip-art, should enable you to prepare some extremely acceptable invitations.

If you have your own computer, there are also software packages on the market that can help you design cards and invitations; there are even specific wedding stationery packages available, so do not be put off! Making your own invitations in this way will save a significant amount of money, and will not take a great deal of time as you will only need to produce one invitation, which can be printed as many times as required.

Cross-stitch cards

If you are handy with a needle, buy blank cards into which a cross-stitch picture can be sewn. However, buy small cards, and make the style a simple one, such as two hearts entwined, or two wedding rings entwined, or you will find yourself completing the last card on your tenth wedding anniversary! Again, the wording will need to be hand-written as these cards are entirely blank.

Floral cards

Dried flowers always look beautiful, even if you are not a great artist. If you have plenty of time, but little money, gather some wild flowers and grasses and press them. After approximately eight weeks, they will be pressed and dry, and can be stuck onto blank cards as used for the cross-stitch invitations.

Photographic cards

Again, purchase some blank cards, and find a romantic picture of the two of you that is small enough to fit into the hole provided. The photograph you choose could be of you both as babies, as children, when you first met, or a funny, serious or romantic picture – the choice is yours. This can be reproduced, and stuck into the card, which can then be personalized with swirls and hearts drawn around the edge of the card with metallic pens. Experiment with scrolls, hearts or just the words 'wedding invitation' on plain paper so that you do not waste any cards.

Calligraphy

If you have beautiful writing, or would like to try calligraphy, there are several 'teach yourself' books on the market to help you. If this appeals, purchase some blank cards, and write a few lines of an appropriate song or poem on the front. Decorate this with a ribbon tied in a bow tied between two punched holes in one corner, or tied down the spine of the invitation.

Other ideas

Simple wording on a sheet of quality paper would be quite acceptable as an invitation. It can be decorated with swirls and hearts drawn with metallic pens, have confetti inserted into the envelope or stuck around the edge of the paper, or even be sprinkled on one corner with a drop of essential oil. The aim is to be different – no-one will realize that this has been done with the aim of cutting costs, but will be impressed by your individuality.

Investigate stationers and art supply shops – the variety of colours and textures of paper available will mean that you will be spoilt for choice.

Haberdashery sections of large department stores stock a wide range of ribbons and bows, particularly during the Christmas season. These can be tied in bows at the corner or bottom of a sheet of paper, or around the spine of a folded card. To maintain the theme, you may even wish to buy extra ribbon to tie the napkins at your reception, and any wedding favours you want to make.

Wedding attire

The bride's dress is usually one of the first items purchased when getting married, and can set her back a great deal of money.

Making the dress

If the bride has sewing skills, or knows a friend or relation who is able to sew the dress, this will save a huge amount of money. Pattern books offer a wide range of styles, but specific patterns may have to be ordered.

Savings can be made by choosing a dress of a simple style. If the bride wishes to have a train to the dress, it is a good idea to find a style with a detachable one, so that the dress can be worn with no train during the dancing at the reception. This would also allow her to wear the dress after the wedding – it could be shortened or dyed to make it more wearable.

Fabric selections are often limited in local stores, and a special trip to London may be required to obtain just the fabric and trimmings desired. The bride should be flexible and open minded in her requirements – if she sees fabric in a sale she may wish to alter her plans, allowing even greater savings on the dress to be made. A good time to look for fabrics for any attendants' dresses is during the pre-Christmas party season; at this time there are lots of velvets, silks and decorative lace that would be suitable and avoid the need to purchase specific bridal silks which tend to be more expensive.

Hiring wedding clothing

Although hiring the wedding dress may not appeal in the first instance, the bride should visit a few bridal shops to see what is on offer. It is worth bearing in mind that the dress will be worn for only a few hours of one day; if the dress chosen costs £900, this could work out at £100 an hour! Hiring is likely to be only one-third of this cost, and the choice of dresses is just as extensive as when buying.

This also applies to bridesmaid's dresses, which can be hired for as little as £45 each. Bridesmaids may prefer to purchase their own dresses; remember that they do not have to be exactly the same style, but should preferably be the same colour. A classic style would also allow the bridesmaids to wear their dress after the wedding.

If the groom and other male members of the bridal party are to wear similar clothing, hiring is also a good option for them. Alternatively, they could wear dark suits that they already own; it is really only necessary for the groom and best man to wear similar clothing if the ushers, etc. already have dark suits. You could make sure they have matching ties and handkerchiefs to tie in with the colour scheme chosen.

Purchasing a gown

Should the bride prefer to purchase a gown, there are still ways to remain cost-conscious. Bridal shops often have sales of gowns, and if the bride is prepared to purchase the dress in good time, she may be able to make good savings on end of season lines.

Another option is to visit the major wedding shows that occur once a year in London, Glasgow and Birmingham; many of the bridal-wear suppliers here sell off their previous season's gowns at less than half price.

If the bride is not in the market for a traditional wedding dress, she could look around at the evening dresses on sale in department stores. Evening dresses in silks, lace and velvet in a wide variety of colours may be more to her taste, and will undoubtedly be much cheaper.

Second-hand dresses

Another good option if the bride wishes to buy a dress is to look in the local newspaper and national wedding magazines. Very often wedding and bridesmaid's dresses are advertized for sale at remarkable reductions from their original sale price.

There are also several second-hand dress agencies and shops around that sell once-worn designer dresses and antique dresses that may be suitable for a wedding.

Other items of clothing

Satin wedding shoes cost a great deal of money, and are invariably not worn again, although they can be dyed another colour for future evening use. If the bride is going to wear a full-length gown, the shoes will not even be seen – so do not feel pressured into buying special shoes.

A cheaper alternative to satin shoes is an elegant white or cream court shoe or sandal. Again, for the very cost conscious, these can be purchased in the end of season sales. These can be worn again, and are therefore more practical.

If the bride wishes to wear a veil, this can also be hired or bought. If she has a friend who has got married before her, she might even be able to borrow theirs. It can be attached in a variety of ways; purchasing a tiara or crown would be the most expensive, but they can also be attached with combs, or pinned in under a circlet of fresh or silk flowers.

A veil is not essential; simple flowers adorning the hair are very effective and are a good option for the budget-conscious bride. She might also like to consider pearl or diamante combs or an Alice band.

Flowers

Choosing flowers in season will always be cheaper than opting for roses or lilies when they are out of season.

The bouquet

Bouquet fashions are changing such that simple ties-bouquets are now more popular than the traditional shower-bouquet. A tied bunch of lilies-of-the-valley, camellia and forget-me-not is an excellent option for a spring bride; if roses are in season, use just a few together with some simple cornflowers for a summer bouquet; use carnations, dahlias, peonies and chrysanthemums for a late summer or early autumn bouquet; a winter bouquet could consist mainly of foliage with some dried flowers and poppyseed pods spray-painted gold.

Even more simple carrying a single rose. If your budget is tight, remember that less is, quite often, more.

You might choose not to carry flowers; a Bible or parasol is a good alternative to the traditional bridal bouquet and can be kept as a memento. Avoid lilies – their pollen is used to make dyes and will indelibly stain any fabric it touches. Avoid daffodils, tulips, gerberas and other flowers with soft, sappy stems – they will almost certainly droop in an hour or so.

Flowers for the attendants

If you are to have small children as attendants at a winter wedding, consider offering them a small muff to wear. This will keep their hands warm and occupied during the ceremony and photographs. For weddings at other times of the year, they may prefer to hold a doll, teddy or hoop rather than flowers.

For country-style weddings, provide bridesmaids with baskets full of fragrant rose petals. These will smell nice during the processional, ceremony and recessional, and can also be sprinkled in front of the couple as they leave the ceremony.

For a simple basket, buy seasonal flowers from a local wholesaler, and arrange them in oasis (a flower-arranging material). Small baskets filled with one type of flower only look very effective.

The ceremony venue

If you are marrying in church, consider asking for the help of their army of helpers who regularly decorate the interior with flowers. If you offer to pay their costs and make a donation to the church for the floral decoration, they may be only too willing to get involved. This could result in a variety of styles being introduced, but if you state the basic colours you would like, you will undoubtedly be impressed by the arrangements, and have far more flowers in the church than you could otherwise afford.

If you are to marry in a hotel or other licensed venue, the floral arrangements may be included in the price, or they may be able to arrange this with their own florist who decorates other areas of the venue.

If the licensed venue is not able to assist with your floral decoration, consider other options. Topiary trees, which would be a good alternative to a large pedestal arrangement, are likely to cost in the region of £60–70. Balloons also offer the same impact as a large flower arrangement but at a much lower cost.

The reception

With small table decorations costing from £14 upwards, you can imagine how your flower bill will soon increase if you have 12 or more tables to decorate. If you elect to have a stand-up buffet, you will immediately cut £160 or more from your florist's bill!

If you wish to have flowers as a table centre, consider growing your own in brightly coloured pots. Hyacinths, daffodils and miniature tulips all look wonderful as living table centres, and have the advantage that they can be given to friends and relatives who have helped with your wedding plans as thank you gifts.

Baskets of dried flowers are also a good way of ensuring greater value for money. The baskets can be used as table centres, and then some kept for your new home, and some given as gifts to those who have assisted with your wedding.

To reduce the number of flowers you need, one good idea is to cover a ball of oasis or florist's foam (available from most florists or craft shops) with flowers, such as chrysanthemums and foliage or dried flowers. Push the ball onto a stick and push into a sprayed or painted flowerpot filled with further oasis. Fill the pot with pebbles to act as a weight.

Glass bowls, shallow, coloured-metal baking tins and ramekin dishes filled with water coloured with food colouring, containing floating candles and flower petals can also look very effective.

One cheap and effective option would be to use nightlights to brighten the table. They can be placed in jars or glasses that have been painted with coloured swirls using glass paint, or that have patterns etched onto the outside with glass etch. If you are dining on trestle tables, try running a line of nightlights in small glass jars (baby-food jars) or in glass or coloured egg cups. Nightlights in egg cups could be used as place markers, with each egg cup having a guest's name painted on it – which can be retained as a memento of the occasion.

Scented candles add yet another dimension to your table centre decorations. Place several on a small plate for most effect.

Bowls filled with fruit make a good decoration if you include a pineapple in the centre, and use star fruit, cape gooseberries and other colourful fruits. This could also provide your dessert, with a chocolate sauce provided for people to dip their chosen fruits.

In winter, a church candle surrounded by nuts, leaves, pinecones and berries looks very effective. Ivy can be draped from the centre between table places. Pinecones can be used to hold your place name tags.

A trio of candles can be placed into inexpensive ironwork candlesticks, and stood at the centre of the table. If the table was then sprinkled with flower petals, or table confetti there would be no need for a flower decoration. White Christmas fairy lights could be used around windows and doors to create a magical feel, and if used with a variety of candles, these may be the only lighting you require for a romantic supper.

Another alternative to flowers is, again, a balloon decoration, which generally costs half as much as the traditional floral table centre. A helium balloon attached to the back of each chair can be used as an unusual, fun place name.

Confetti sprinkled over the table, and streamers running across the top between table settings are another colourful, cheap and effective way of decorating. The streamers can also be used around the room, and hung over the backs of chairs.

If you keep the table centres simple, you can afford to be imaginative with other areas of presentation. For example, if you are using a fruit arrangement as the centrepiece, which will double as your dessert, why not use fruit to display your menu card; it can be tied with ribbon and slotted between the fruits, pinned to oranges, limes or lemons to give a wonderful citrus smell, or tied to banana leaves or large variegated laurel leaves with ribbons.

Place name cards can also be pinned to fruits; they can be slotted into napkins tied up with grasses, hessian or ribbon or tied with ribbon to cutlery. Cheap luggage labels can also be used and tied to the backs of chairs.

A large decorative shell, filled with seasonal flowers, and surrounded with pebbles would make an unusual table decoration. Place names could be painted onto larger pebbles. This would be an appropriate decoration for anyone living by the sea, or serving a fish starter, which could be waiting for guests as they arrive.

Photography

One important thing to remember about your wedding photographs is that you will have them for the rest of your life. If you would like a professional photographer, but feel that the cost is too great, employ the best that you can but use their minimum service – which should cover leaving the bride's home, the formal photographs before and after the ceremony and up to the cutting of the cake. This will give you many photographs from which to choose an album of approximately 25 to 30.

Alternatively, you could provide some of your guests who you know are keen photographers with a film each before the day. They will be able to take more relaxed photographs, and may even catch a gem or two that will make your day really special.

A good way of recording parts of the reception that you may not otherwise get to see is by providing each table with a disposable camera. These can be purchased by mail order from several companies that will print them with your names and the date of the wedding, or you may choose the cheaper option of a standard single-use camera.

Videography

You may feel that having a video of your wedding is an essential part of the memory of your big day; however, it may be a luxury that you ultimately cannot afford.

Some videographers are able to produce stills from a video that they take; you may feel that this would be a better option, and would mean that you need not employ a photographer – which would undoubtedly save money overall. However, if you decide to consider this option, choose your videographer carefully, and ensure that you see samples, including stills, of his or her work in advance.

With the popularity of camcorders, you might find that you have a willing friend who is able to video your wedding. This is often more fun as it will be produced showing warts and all!

Transport

With the help of friends, you might find that you can cut this expenditure entirely from your budget, or use only one car. If anyone in the family has a suitable car, arrange to have it valet-cleaned and buy a length of white ribbon to tie from the front windows to the front grill. Your flowers can be used to decorate the back window on your journey to the ceremony, and on to the reception.

If you decide to hire only one wedding car, and the journey is a short distance from your home, the same car can be used to transport the mother of the bride and the bridesmaids before returning to collect the bride and her father. Alternatively, you might have access to a friend's car that may be used for the bridesmaids, and so could reserve the wedding car for the bride. This will cut the cost of your transport in half.

Another alternative to hiring a traditional wedding car is to arrange for a standard taxi to collect you. This gives you the convenience of being driven without the expense of a wedding car.

If you have a large wedding party, why not hire a bus? If you have several people travelling from a distance who will be staying overnight at a local hotel, what better way to get into the party mood than by travelling to the wedding together in a bus bedecked with balloons and streamers – and then, on from the ceremony to the reception. This will solve all the problems of parking, and those not wishing to drink and drive!

Hire of reception venue

Some venues may charge many thousands of pounds to hire their venue. This is an area in which you may be able to make a large saving, either by using a hotel that will not charge, as their fee is within the cost of the food, or by hiring a local village hall or community centre.

Very often halls such as this are extremely good value for money, but watch out for extras, such as heating that is operational by coin meter, and hire of tables and chairs. Halls also offer you complete freedom as to how you cater for your event – if you wish to cater for yourself, check the kitchen facilities. You are also offered a totally blank canvas on which to develop your decorations to your own personal taste. You will generally have access to the hall for more than just the day itself, and can prepare the room the day before the event, thus spreading the work required to set up the reception.

Another option is to hold the reception at home or in your garden. Other options may include the beach or local picnic beauty spot, depending upon the style of party you want.

If you have a smaller party, your local public house may be just the place to hold your reception. They may be prepared to close off the restaurant for your party only, and pub food is generally of a good standard and excellent value for money.

Catering and food

Again, this is another area that can vary enormously. The cheapest way of engaging caterers is for them to provide a sandwich buffet or canapés for a cocktail party. The most expensive is a three-course, sit-down banquet. The choice of catering depends upon the time of day that the wedding is to take place. Also, if you have a limited budget, it is better to limit the number of guests and the length of the reception rather than try to have a grand affair on a shoestring.

If the wedding is to take place at 11 a.m. or midday, guests will expect to get a meal. Either a sit-down, two-course meal or a stand-up buffet would be suitable at this time of day.

For early risers; why not get married early in the morning – don't forget you can marry as early as 8 a.m. – and have a true wedding breakfast! A breakfast or brunch including Eggs Benedict, scrambled eggs and smoked salmon, kedgeree, muffins, bagels, freshly baked bread and lots of freshly squeezed juices would be good value for money, and make for a very original reception. And don't forget the buck's fizz to toast the happy couple!

If the wedding is to take place early in the afternoon, an 'afternoon tea' would be appropriate, serving sandwiches and cake at between 4 p.m. and 5 p.m. This form of catering is not as common as other forms of wedding breakfast, and should therefore be referred to on the invitation so that guests know what to expect. For example, you could write: '... and afterwards for afternoon tea at ...'

Another good way of reducing the cost would be to hold a cocktail reception. This would be appropriate for those marrying later in the afternoon, with champagne or sparkling wine and canapés served at 6.30–6 p.m. Be inventive and find a caterer that is able to provide a Spanish tapas, or Eastern Mediterranean mezze. Again, guests should be made aware of the plans. Such a reception would finish by 8 p.m. so that guests can then leave and dine at their own convenience. If you wish, you may continue with a formal dinner to which only close family and friends are invited. This will allow you to spend the lion's share of your budget on those people that mean most to you.

The afternoon tea and cocktail reception options also allow you to cut the band or disco from your budget.

If you wish to employ a caterer, be honest about your budget. They will be able to advise you on the best way to deal with feeding your guests.

Hotel catering is generally much less flexible. Generally speaking, they have standard banqueting menus from which to choose the style of reception that you want, either stand-up buffet, carved buffet or banquet. If asked, they may be able to provide you with a set-budget menu. It is worth asking around several hotels as their prices do vary. With cheaper menus, do check for hidden extras, such as room hire charges, and corkage.

The cheapest form of catering would be either to do it yourself, either partially or totally. However, be prepared for a lot of work, and don't try to do anything too difficult.

A barbecue or hog roast is an excellent choice for venues that are set in attractive grounds, and are very good value for money. You may have friends who are prepared to pitch in to do the barbecue, whilst you have accompanying dishes prepared by other family members. If you would prefer a hog roast, there are several excellent companies that specialize in this type of catering, and are generally able to supply all the accompanying dishes.

A good idea for self-catering is to ask your local butcher to cook a whole ham for you, and to carve it off the bone. Cook a couple of large turkeys, which are available frozen throughout the year now, and also carve these off the bone. Add to this a selection of salads and chunks of bread, freshly baked from your local bakery, and you have a basic buffet. Follow this with a dessert of fresh fruit salad accompanied by meringues or shortbread fingers and you have a simple meal to be proud of.

Another option would be to serve old favourites such as bangers and mash or fish and chips. You might even consider hiring a fish and chip van to cater for you!

Drink

Don't feel that you have to serve champagne; a good sparkling wine is better than a cheap champagne any day. Most wine companies offer good quality wines on a sale or return basis, and you will be able to try them before you buy.

With the advent of the Channel Tunnel link, some couples make a trip to France a few weeks prior to their wedding. The supermarkets on the other side of the tunnel stock the same wines as they do in this country at a fraction of the cost; find a few that you like by buying them in advance and trying them before you go so that you are sure of what you are getting.

Supermarkets in the United Kingdom are also a good option for purchase of wines; they very often provide glasses free of charge, and any wine that is not used can often be returned after the event.

At the reception you should also offer plenty of mineral water and fruit juices so that people do not feel duty-bound to drink wine. There is a wealth of flavoured mineral waters on the market now that make an excellent alternative to standard soft drinks.

If you would like to offer a cheaper alternative to sherry or champagne as your guests arrive, you could offer Pimms or sangria during the summer, or mulled wine at a winter wedding.

If you wish to offer a wider selection of alcoholic drinks, hire an outside bar service. They can provide a full bar service that can either be charged to your guests as drinks are purchased, or you can ask that a record is kept of drinks consumed for the bill to be settled at the end of the reception. Beware – people will drink more when they know it is free!

Cake

The cake might seem like an important consideration; however, most people only see the small piece on their plate at the reception, and the photographs afterwards.

Consider having a single-tier sponge cake iced in the traditional manner, and used for the 'cutting of the cake' part of the reception. Behind the scenes, you could also have a traditional cake which is top-iced only, with no fancy decoration. After the sponge cake is removed, both cakes can be cut and offered to guests at the end of the reception. This will, surprisingly, cut the cost of your cake virtually in half.

Another option is to have a French wedding cake, or *croquembouche*. This is a pile of profiterole-style buns, filled with cream and covered with spun sugar. It can also be decorated with fresh flowers. This would serve not only as the cake, but also as dessert, cutting the overall cost of catering.

Do you or other members of your family make Christmas cakes? A wedding cake is no more difficult than that! Once the cake is flat-iced, you can obtain all sorts of decorative items as a finishing touch – from a plastic bride and groom, to ribbons, bows and sugar flowers. These can be sourced from specialist cake-decorating shops, and good stationers. Cake stands can be hired from catering equipment hire companies, some of which have stands on different levels so that the cakes do not have to be placed on top of each other in tiers. This is an excellent idea if you are worried that the cake will not turn out entirely flat on top!

If you are not confident of your abilities, you might wish to combine the two suggestions above, by having a single-tier cake made professionally, with a home-baked cake, top-iced only, for cutting behind the scenes.

Going-away outfits

Do not be tempted to buy an outfit that you will never wear again. If you are leaving your reception late in the evening, you may even have to put a coat over what you are wearing in any case, so nobody will see your outfit!

If the bride or groom really want to buy something new, buy something practical – there is no need to spend a great deal of money. For example, if the bride usually lives in trousers, a comfortable new pair and a special silky blouse is all that is needed. She needn't bother with a hat – she will probably never wear it again and it is bound to cost at least £50.

If the bride's dress is a simple shift style, she needn't bother with a going-away outfit at all. She can simply slip a warm wrap over her shoulders and be ready to leave the party for her first night of wedded bliss!

First-night hotel

This may be the one area that you do not wish to skimp upon. The first night of your married life is special, and you will want to spend it in luxurious surroundings. However, several extremely good bed and breakfast establishments may well fit this category. Do your homework and you should be able to find a good deal.

Honeymoon

This is an area in which you can save a huge amount of money. You needn't think that you have to go to some far-flung place that you would never normally plan to visit. Do you really want to have the effects of malaria tablets, injections and the like making you feel down just before your wedding, when you already have enough to worry about?

Holidaying in Europe, or even the United Kingdom, will provide you with just as much peace and relaxation as going further afield. Holidaying in Greece, Spain or other such popular destinations will give you the good weather, without being too distant, or very expensive.

The idea of the honeymoon is to get away to relax after all the hectic preparations of the weeks leading up to your wedding. A long flight and jet lag may not be the best way to recover!

Another way to spread the cost of your wedding is to honeymoon sometime after the wedding date itself, for example, to combine it with your summer break. This will give you time to settle down after all the excitement, get used to married life, and still give you something to look forward to. Often the period just after a wedding feels a little strange – you have spent so many hours planning and preparing, and you now have nothing to do in the evenings. It may take a little time to adjust to the comparative inactivity, and delaying your honeymoon will give you something to look forward to.

Weddings on a budget

So where does this leave you? If you wish to use a selection of the ideas used above, and restrict your guest list to 50 people, you can expect to reduce the cost of your wedding to less than half the average figure mentioned above, as follows:

Item	Budget
Stationery – computer package, textured paper and ribbon for invitations, envelopes, menus, order of service and place name cards	60
Bride's dress – hired from local bridal agency	130
Bridesmaid's dresses – two hired from a local bridal agency	120
Groom and best man suit hire, shirt and tie purchase	130
Bride's plain 19ct gold band wedding ring	80
Groom's plain 19ct gold band wedding ring	80
Flowers	150
Church fees	125
Photography – minimum package, plus four films, and six disposable cameras	350
Video	None
Transport – friend's car (for ribbons only)	20
Hire of reception room – free within a hotel. Local village hall/community centre	50
Catering and food – sandwich and snacks buffet at £10 per head	500
Drink – two glasses of wine per person, one glass sparkling wine, purchased on sale or return basis. Pay bar.	200
Cake – single-layer iced sponge, one fruit cake top-iced only	100
Disco	200
Bride's going-away outfit	70
First-night hotel	120
Honeymoon – self-catering in Greece/Spanish islands	1,200
Total cost	£3,685

The secret of sticking to your budget is to decide which areas of the wedding are important to you, and which are not. Then you can spend the money on things that you consider important, and save in other areas.

Do not be afraid to ask for help with the cost of your wedding by asking for something that you need as a wedding gift. If you have a friend or relative who is excellent at making cakes, ask them to provide you with a wedding cake as a gift; if someone you know has a suitable car, ask if they could drive it for you on the day as their wedding present. People will be only too pleased to help, and not at all offended. They will be pleased to think that they can provide you with something that nobody else can, rather than just another set of towels or glasses!

10 after the wedding

Americans have a saying 'the game ain't over 'til the fat lady sings' which is a reference to the end of a baseball game when an operatic diva sings the US national anthem before the crowd disperses to go home. You may not have an operatic diva at your beck and call, but there are still several things that need attention after the wedding day before it can be said that the 'game' is over.

Saying 'thank you'

Thank you is such a small thing to say, but the effect it has on the recipient far outweighs the small effort needed to say it. The bride's parents are the first on the list for thanks because, even in these days of less-rigid etiquette, when many other people lend a hand, most of the burden of planning and expense generally falls on them.

A week or so after the newly-weds return from honeymoon, when the dust has settled, they may like to consider ways of showing their appreciation to the bride's parents. There are lots of ways to say thank you; a pair of theatre tickets, a day out, dinner at their favourite restaurant or, perhaps, the bridal bouquet, dried, pressed and mounted, as a gift would be appropriate.

The best man and other attendants will have already received a small gift from the bride and groom to thank them for everything they have done but a short note, or a card, when they return from their honeymoon will round things off nicely.

The groom's parents may also warrant a thank you, especially if they have done more than generally expected to encourage and support their son throughout the planning stages. As with the bride's parents, theatre tickets, dinner at a favourite restaurant or a day out somewhere should be well received.

The less obvious recipients of thanks include the minister/priest or registrar who officiated at the ceremony, with a special mention for the organist, choir and bellringer's leaders, if appropriate, and the hotel staff or caterers who looked after the reception. People such as the cake-maker, florist, and chauffeur will all value being remembered with thanks.

Others to receive a handwritten thank you note are those who sent or brought a gift for the newly-weds. Gifts which were received before the wedding should have been acknowledged as soon as they arrived and those which arrived at the reception, or since, should be acknowledged as soon as possible afterwards.

Clearing up

Hired outfits should have been returned to the hiring company by the chief bridesmaid/matron-of-honour, the best man or whoever the task has been delegated to by the bride and groom. This messenger should also have collected any deposits and returned them to whoever paid them, but the newly-weds might like to check, just to be sure.

Most hotel function co-ordinators and hall managers will contact clients to tell them if any lost property was found when the room was cleared after a wedding reception, but, again, a phone call to check is always worthwhile.

If a complete tier of the wedding cake is still intact now is the time to store it for a future occasion if you wish. If it is to be stored, find a close-fitting, empty, cake or biscuit box, or an airtight polythene storage box, making sure it is scrupulously clean and perfectly dry. Line with layers of greaseproof paper and place the cake inside. Remove any decorations and ribbons or flowers, layer more paper around, and on top of the cake, fit the lid and store the box somewhere cool and completely free from condensation or damp of any kind.

A well-made fruit cake should keep for a very long time, in the right conditions, although the icing may discolour a little and the cake may not be quite as moist as when it was new. This can be corrected by taking off the old icing, adding some moisture (a little brandy, perhaps) and re-icing.

> An interesting story tells of a couple who contacted the bakery where their wedding cake was made, asking if they could replace slightly discoloured icing on the top tier so they could use it at the baptism of their first child. It was only later that the staff at the bakery discovered it was to be an adult baptism and the child was, in fact, 17 years old! Apparently the cake was delicious!

Photograph and video selection

The photographer and video maker should have the results of their work ready for the couple to look at when they arrive back from their honeymoon. The couple will be able to choose a selection from the photographs, for inclusion in the wedding album.

It is not obligatory to buy an album offered by the photographer, even if the price already includes the album, and there are many designs and types of book available at any good photographic retailers. Some albums are designed as complete record books, having pages on which to record the guest list, gifts received, and so on. However, part of the photographer's profit comes from the onward sale of albums so he or she is unlikely to give much of a discount should the couple decide to buy their album elsewhere. The cost of your package should entitle you to keep all the photograph proofs but not the negatives or the copyright. Proofs will not be final quality, and are not suitable for framing or including in the album, but will allow you to look through the pictures and choose additional copies later, if you so wish. Ask the photographer how long he or she will hold the negatives, and whether you can reorder after a period of time, say a year or even longer.

Remember, although you may keep the proofs, the photographer has copyright title and if you copy the pictures yourself, even on a photocopier, you will be breaking the law and the photographer can sue, if he or she chooses.

Copyright laws almost certainly apply to the video as well as to photographs but this is unlikely to cause any real problems since wedding videos generally appeal only to those most closely involved with the bride and groom, so fewer copies are needed.

Flower and dress preservation

Wedding services directories in magazines, *Yellow Pages* and craft fairs are all good sources of craftspeople who do this sort of work. For flower preservation, the flowers will need to be looked after very well on the wedding day, preferably sprayed with clear water as soon as the bride arrives at the reception and stored somewhere very cool during the celebrations and, if necessary, overnight.

They should be delivered to the company or person engaged to do the work as quickly as possible, which means someone should be delegated to deliver them in the bride's absence. Some people working in this field operate a mail order service, in which case they will advise on how to deliver the flowers to them in good condition. Check with the company concerned well in advance. Drying can take several weeks, so don't expect instant results.

There are fewer companies specializing in the preservation of wedding dresses. If *Yellow Pages* has no listing, bridal magazines should be able to help. Some companies supply a box made specially for the purpose and a set of instructions on how to store the dress: others will ask for the dress to be delivered to them and will return it wrapped and packed ready for storage.

Every wedding dress will eventually deteriorate if stored incorrectly, and, once discolouration has occurred, it is impossible to remove. After the wedding, the dress should be expertly cleaned, hung in the fresh air for an hour or so to let every remaining trace of dry cleaning fluid evaporate, then placed inside a natural cotton bag which is long enough to take the full length of the dress without creases.

If possible, the dress should be stored flat, inside the cotton bag, but if this is not possible, it may be hung from a well-padded hanger somewhere high enough to prevent it trailing on the floor and with enough space so that it is not crushed. Stored this way, most dresses will be perfectly all right for several months but a more permanent home will be needed eventually, even if only to release much-needed wardrobe space.

Complaints

If there is any cause to complain either to, or about, any of the traders who supplied services to the wedding, now is the time to do it. If it is an item covered under the wedding insurance package, complete and send off a claim as soon as possible.

If the nature of the complaint puts it outside the terms of insurance cover, a complaint to the trader concerned should always be in writing stating clearly the nature of the problem, what happened, what was done (if anything) to try to put it right at the time and what the company is expected to do about it now.

Getting back any money paid, or an amount in compensation, is almost always difficult but, if the case is a good one, it should be possible to pursue it through the Small Claims Court at the local county court. Neighbourhood advice centres, Citizen's Advice Bureaux or the county court office, all listed in the telephone directory, will be able to advise on how to go about this.

With these loose ends tied up, your wedding day is now truly over. The problems and frustrations of planning will soon fade away to nothing, but the photographs, the video and your memories will stay with you all your life.

Your future

The big difference between moving in with someone and marrying them is commitment, commitment that allows and encourages a long-term view and planning for a future that two people will share. Being newly married is the perfect opportunity for reviewing existing plans and making new ones. Here we look at a few of the issues which are often uppermost in the minds of newly-weds and consider what they may mean to you.

Financial planning

Many people sail through life without any help at all from the people who are now called financial planners, or consultants, and manage very well. Nevertheless, there are situations where expert help and advice is useful and, occasionally, essential.

Buying a home, taking out a loan, planning a pension, insuring a life and investing in stocks and shares are just a few of the many financial issues with which people become involved. The list is long, including endowments for children's education fees, insurance for personal accident and motor cover, self-employment, business planning, and so on.

Personal financial planning can take some of the chance elements out of life, providing a fall-back position in the event of illness or accident, ensure a comfortable retirement and take care of dependants in the event of death. Traditionally, these plans have been male preserves, mostly because women have been unlikely to have the income on which planning depends. Nowadays, however, more and more women have their own incomes and more and more households are dependent on two incomes in order to maintain a desired lifestyle. Who should plan for what, and when, are the two key factors that planners are equipped to identify.

There are two entirely different types of financial planners, and the difference is crucial to those in the market place for the first time. First, are the tied agents who work as employees or agents of specific companies. They are able to compare the products which their own company markets with those of other, similar, companies but, apart from pension advice, they are not obliged to give impartial advice on which is best for a specific client. They are bound, by their contracts of employment, always to present and recommend the products of their own company, but are also obliged to explain this to potential clients at the outset of discussions.

Independent advisers are able to research different companies in the field to find the product that best suits their clients' needs, with no bias to any specific company. They will then advise which company and which product will satisfy the clients' needs best.

There are advantages and drawbacks to each. For example, the tied employee or agent has a vested interest in securing as much of your business as possible for his or her employers because his or her income, and perhaps job, rests on continuing success.

For the independent, who still relies on clients and business volume for his/her income, there is more freedom to manoeuvre because commission will be earned from whichever company receives the business he or she writes. Even here, however, there may well be constraints on impartiality because some companies pay more commission than others.

As a client, the potential buyer of services, deciding which company to use can be a thought-provoking decision but it need not be difficult. Buying financial advice is not much different from buying any other product – be clear about what you want, ask the relevant questions, listen carefully to the answers and buy what suits you best.

Gender issues

Marriage today is a rather different institution from even just a few years ago and much different from those marriages on which our parents embarked. Even so, in spite of all the challenges to gender roles which have been addressed in the past few years, some of the traditional attitudes remain.

Social studies continually show that it is the female partner who carries the greater part of the burden of childcare and homemaking in the majority of marriages and partnerships and, where there are children, the death or incapacity of the wife/mother can have a far greater financial impact on the family than the absence or incapacity of the husband/father.

It follows, therefore, that any financial planning for the family should include provision for the female partner in at least the same measure as for the male and, perhaps, even more.

Making a will

Making a will is almost universally seen as being a morbid task which only 'older' people need to worry about. Nothing could be further than from the truth. It is an act of love and caring, undertaken by those who wish to spare their loved ones the added pain of worry and, perhaps, hardship when they die, especially if that death is premature and unexpected.

Everyone has an 'estate', the term given to property, goods and money left behind by the deceased. It may be property and wealth amounting to millions of pounds, or a modest home, car and a few personal possessions. Without a will, it can be months, and sometimes years, before those left behind are able to gain access to the bank account that paid the bills, the savings that were to pay for a holiday or even the insurance money that was to pay the mortgage.

Making a will is, for most people, a simple thing to do, involving a few minutes with a solicitor or a professional will writer. In most cases costs are modest and the will is ready within a few days. Once completed, it can be tucked away somewhere safe and will be needed again on only a few occasions when circumstances suggest an updating would be advisable, such as on the birth of a child or a substantial change of financial worth – for example, hitting the jackpot on the National Lottery!

Marriage automatically invalidates any will made earlier. This will be of particular relevance and importance to people marrying later in life or those entering a second or subsequent marriage. They may have existing responsibilities, acquired before the marriage, which need to be discharged and protected after their death and making a will ensures that their wishes are carried out promptly and without confusion.

Changing a name

The majority of married women change their last name to that of their husband on marriage without realizing that, although this is the custom and practice, it is not obligatory in the United Kingdom. A married woman is entitled to use either her own name, or that of her husband, or a mixture of both, as she wishes.

Last names can be changed by deed poll, as well as by marriage, but, in law, a person has the right to use, and be known by, any last name they please providing there is no intent to deceive or defraud. This means that a signature on a legally binding agreement, such as a mortgage or passport application, must be the name at birth, the name adopted on marriage or by deed poll, of the person to whom it relates.

If a married woman retains her former name after marriage, she may find it creates confusion at times, especially when travelling abroad. She may wish to carry a copy of her marriage certificate at such times.

Against this inconvenience, a married woman will often need to balance the advantages of keeping her own name. If she has already built, or is building, a flourishing career, a change of name can have serious effects where her reputation is linked with her name but where she is not, personally, known. In large organizations, where reputations travel ahead of the face, this could be a significant problem.

First names are different. One must, in law, always use the first name registered at birth, unless the whole name is changed by deed poll.

Finale

Contrary to much popular opinion, a wedding isn't the end of anything (except, perhaps, wedding planning!) but a new beginning, and everything new involves changes and adjustments. Mostly, these first few months after marriage are a time of discovery and revelation as you get to know each other and sort out your priorities.

Financial planning, property and all the other big decisions don't need to be addressed right away, in fact they are probably best left for a while until you are more comfortable with each other.

We hope you have found this book helpful and informative, and perhaps you will recommend it to friends when it is their turn to marry: maybe you will put it with your wedding album as a keepsake and show it to your own children when it is their turn to marry – it may be a source of great amusement 20 years from now! Whatever your plans, we wish you good luck for your future together and may your married life be prosperous and happy.

taking it further

Useful addresses

Copies of birth and/or adoption certificates and death certificates may be obtained from:

General Register Office
for England and Wales
Family Records Office
Smedley Hydro
Trafalgar Road
Birkdale
Southport
Merseyside
PR8 2HH
Tel: 01704 569824

The Registrar General
for England and Wales
Office of Population,
Census' and Surveys
St Catherine's House
10 Kingsway
London WC2B 6JP
Tel: 0171 242 0262

General Register Office for
Northern Ireland
Oxford House
49–55 Chichester Street
Belfast BT1 4HL
Tel: 01232 235211

General Register Office
for Scotland
New Register House
Edinburgh EH1 3YT
Tel: 0131 334 0380

General Register Office
for the Isle of Man
Finch Road
Douglas
Isle of Man
Tel: 01624 5212

Register General
for Guernsey
The Greffe
Royal Court House
St Peter Port
Guernsey
Tel: 01481 725277

Civil/religious contacts

Catholic ceremonies
Catholic Marriage Advisory
Council
Clitherow House
1 Blythe Mews
Blythe Road
London W14 0NW

Celtic ministers
The Pagan Federation
Box 7097
London SW1N 3XX

Foreign and Commonwealth Office
The Nationality Treaty &
Claims Department
Clive House
Petty France
London SW1H 9HD
Tel: (020) 7238 4567

Freelance minister
Rev Jonathan Blake
Whispering Trees
273 Beechings Way
Gillingham
Kent ME8 7BP

Humanist ceremonies
British Humanist Association
47 Theobald's Road
London W1X 8SP

Jewish ceremonies
Jewish Marriage Council
23 Ravenshurst Avenue
London NW4 4EE

Union of Liberal and
Progressive Synagogues
The Montagu Centre
21 Mapel Street
London W1P 7DS

Office for National Statistics
Trafalgar Road
Southport PR8 2HH

For overseas marriage enquiries
General Register Office
Overseas Section
Smedley Hydro
Trafalgar Road
Southport PR8 2HH

Quaker ceremonies
Quakers (The Religious
Society of Friends)
Friends House
173–177 Euston Road
London NW1 2BJ

Scottish weddings
Church of Scotland
121 George Street
Edinburgh EH2 4YN

Single-sex unions
Lesbian and Gay Christian
Movement
Oxford House
Derbyshire Street
London E2 6HG

Metropolitan Community
Church
2A Sistova Road
Balham
London SW12 9QT

Unitarian ceremonies
Unitarian Church
Essex Hall
1–6 Essex Street
London WC2R 3HY

Other addresses

These addresses are merely suggestions of what is available and are by no means exhaustive. For details of what is available in your area consult the Corporate Entertainment section of your local *Yellow Pages* directory.

Celtic headdresses
Sophie Jonas
Brook House Design Studio
Bluebridge Road
Brookmans Park
Hatfield AL9 7SX

National theatrical costumier/ private hire
Royal Exchange Costume Hire
Royal Exchange Theatre
St Anne's Square
Manchester M2 5DH

Party shops
Peeks Party Store
Reid Street
Fairmile Road
Christchurch
Dorset BH23 2BT

Period and themed stationery
The Oliver Collection
Pondu House
Mylor Harbour
Falmouth
Cornwall TR11 5UG
Tel: 01326 373649

Specialist vehicle hire
For vehicles from all periods
Carriages Vehicle Agency
147 Nork Way
Banstead
Surrey SM7 1HR

Wedding co-ordination and events management
Dianne ffitch
Days to Remember
36 Church Road
Otley
Ipswich IP6 9NP
Tel: 01473 890964
Fax: 01473 890412
email:
  enquiries@daystoremember.co.uk
Website:
  www.daystoremember.co.uk

Books

Your local library can provide wonderful sources of inspiration and ideas for themes for your wedding day.

index

teach® yourself

Afrikaans
Access 2002
Accounting, Basic
Alexander Technique
Algebra
Arabic
Arabic Script, Beginner's
Aromatherapy
Astronomy
Bach Flower Remedies
Bengali
Better Chess
Better Handwriting
Biology
Body Language
Book Keeping
Book Keeping & Accounting
Brazilian Portuguese
Bridge
Buddhism
Buddhism, 101 Key Ideas
Bulgarian
Business Studies
Business Studies, 101 Key Ideas
C++
Calculus
Calligraphy
Cantonese
Card Games
Catalan
Chemistry, 101 Key Ideas
Chess
Chi Kung
Chinese
Chinese, Beginner's

Chinese Language, Life & Culture
Chinese Script, Beginner's
Christianity
Classical Music
Copywriting
Counselling
Creative Writing
Crime Fiction
Croatian
Crystal Healing
Czech
Danish
Desktop Publishing
Digital Photography
Digital Video & PC Editing
Drawing
Dream Interpretation
Dutch
Dutch, Beginner's
Dutch Dictionary
Dutch Grammar
Eastern Philosophy
ECDL
E-Commerce
Economics, 101 Key Ideas
Electronics
English, American (EFL)
English as a Foreign Language
English, Correct
English Grammar
English Grammar (EFL)
English, Instant, for French Speakers
English, Instant, for German Speakers
English, Instant, for Italian Speakers
English, Instant, for Spanish Speakers

English for International Business
English Language, Life & Culture
English Verbs
English Vocabulary
Ethics
Excel 2002
Feng Shui
Film Making
Film Studies
Finance for non-Financial Managers
Finnish
Flexible Working
Flower Arranging
French
French, Beginner's
French Grammar
French Grammar, Quick Fix
French, Instant
French, Improve your
French Language, Life & Culture
French Starter Kit
French Verbs
French Vocabulary
Gaelic
Gaelic Dictionary
Gardening
Genetics
Geology
German
German, Beginner's
German Grammar
German Grammar, Quick Fix
German, Instant
German, Improve your
German Language, Life & Culture
German Verbs
German Vocabulary
Go
Golf
Greek
Greek, Ancient
Greek, Beginner's
Greek, Instant
Greek, New Testament
Greek Script, Beginner's
Guitar
Gulf Arabic
Hand Reflexology
Hebrew, Biblical
Herbal Medicine
Hieroglyphics
Hindi
Hindi, Beginner's
Hindi Script, Beginner's

Hinduism
History, 101 Key Ideas
How to Win at Horse Racing
How to Win at Poker
HTML Publishing on the WWW
Human Anatomy & Physiology
Hungarian
Icelandic
Indian Head Massage
Indonesian
Information Technology, 101 Key Ideas
Internet, The
Irish
Islam
Italian
Italian, Beginner's
Italian Grammar
Italian Grammar, Quick Fix
Italian, Instant
Italian, Improve your
Italian Language, Life & Culture
Italian Verbs
Italian Vocabulary
Japanese
Japanese, Beginner's
Japanese, Instant
Japanese Language, Life & Culture
Japanese Script, Beginner's
Java
Jewellery Making
Judaism
Korean
Latin
Latin American Spanish
Latin, Beginner's
Latin Dictionary
Latin Grammar
Letter Writing Skills
Linguistics
Linguistics, 101 Key Ideas
Literature, 101 Key Ideas
Mahjong
Managing Stress
Marketing
Massage
Mathematics
Mathematics, Basic
Media Studies
Meditation
Mosaics
Music Theory
Needlecraft
Negotiating
Nepali

Norwegian
Origami
Panjabi
Persian, Modern
Philosophy
Philosophy of Mind
Philosophy of Religion
Philosophy of Science
Philosophy, 101 Key Ideas
Photography
Photoshop
Physics
Piano
Planets
Planning Your Wedding
Polish
Politics
Portuguese
Portuguese, Beginner's
Portuguese Grammar
Portuguese, Instant
Portuguese Language, Life & Culture
Postmodernism
Pottery
Powerpoint 2002
Presenting for Professionals
Project Management
Psychology
Psychology, 101 Key Ideas
Psychology, Applied
Quark Xpress
Quilting
Recruitment
Reflexology
Reiki
Relaxation
Retaining Staff
Romanian
Russian
Russian, Beginner's
Russian Grammar
Russian, Instant
Russian Language, Life & Culture
Russian Script, Beginner's
Sanskrit
Screenwriting
Serbian
Setting up a Small Business
Shorthand, Pitman 2000
Sikhism
Spanish
Spanish, Beginner's
Spanish Grammar
Spanish Grammar, Quick Fix

Spanish, Instant
Spanish, Improve your
Spanish Language, Life & Culture
Spanish Starter Kit
Spanish Verbs
Spanish Vocabulary
Speaking on Special Occasions
Speed Reading
Statistical Research
Statistics
Swahili
Swahili Dictionary
Swedish
Tagalog
Tai Chi
Tantric Sex
Teaching English as a Foreign Language
Teaching English One to One
Teams and Team-Working
Thai
Time Management
Tracing your Family History
Travel Writing
Trigonometry
Turkish
Turkish, Beginner's
Typing
Ukrainian
Urdu
Urdu Script, Beginner's
Vietnamese
Volcanoes
Watercolour Painting
Weight Control through Diet and
  Exercise
Welsh
Welsh Dictionary
Welsh Language, Life & Culture
Wills and Probate
Wine Tasting
Winning at Job Interviews
Word 2002
World Faiths
Writing a Novel
Writing for Children
Writing Poetry
Xhosa
Yoga
Zen
Zulu

teach yourself

speaking on special occasions
roger mason

- Are you worried about making a speech?
- Do you want to know where to begin and what to cover?
- Would you like examples of what works?

Speaking on Special Occasions explains how to plan and make a good speech, whatever the occasion. It will give you strategies for dealing with nerves and building your confidence, so that both you and your audience enjoy your speech.

Roger Mason is an experienced speaker and writer.

teach
yourself

better handwriting

rosemary sassoon & gunnlaugur se briem

- Do you want to improve your handwriting technique?
- Do you experience problems with writing and want help?
- Are you looking to experiment and develop your own style?

Better Handwriting is a practical and informative guide. The way we write mirrors our mood and character. It is the way we project ourselves to the world – and other people often judge us by our handwriting. This book is specifically written for adults and will help you to improve and develop a mature and individual style.

Rosemary Sassoon is a letterform consultant specializing in the educational and medical aspects of handwriting. She has a PhD from Reading University. **Gunnlaugur SE Briem** is an Icelandic designer and has a PhD from the Royal College of Art in London.

teach
yourself

letter writing skills

david james with anthony masters

- Do you want to write clear, persuasive letters?
- Do you want to communicate more confidently?
- Do you need to update your letter-writing style?

Letter Writing Skills is an invaluable guide to writing letters which say exactly what you want to say – and bring the desired response. It offers practical advice on layout, style and tone and examines different types of letter, from personal to business correspondence. A section on electronic communication helps you to make the most of email.

David Masters is a writer of both adult and children's fiction and non-fiction books. He also runs writing workshops for adults and children.

teach yourself

tracing your family history
stella colwell

- Are you new to genealogy?
- Do you want to find right sources quickly and easily?
- Do you need guidance to improve your skills?

Tracing your Family History is a practical and comprehensive guide to genealogy. It covers everything you need to trace your family's history, from planning your research to interviewing your relatives effectively, and gives detailed guidance on finding and using the right basic sources for tracing births, marriages and deaths, pointing you in the direction of other linked records to help build up the picture of your family's past.

Stella Colwell is the Family and Local History Specialist Reader Adviser at the Public Record Office, Kew. She has lectured and taught weekend courses worldwide.

teach yourself

wills and probate
jacqueline martin & richard pooley

- Do you want to know more about wills and inheritance?
- Do you want help with legal terminology?
- Do you want to be sure that your wishes are clear and binding?

Wills and Probate gives you comprehensive guidance on making a will, probate and the rules of inheritance. It explains what happens to property when there is no will and gives practical advice on what to do when someone dies. It contains a glossary of legal expressions and separate chapters for the rules in Scotland and Northern Ireland.

Jacqueline Martin is a barrister and **Richard Pooley** is a solicitor and lecturer.